Unto thee I grant

Revised by
Sri. Ramatherio
a private, limited edition

ROSICRUCIAN LIBRARY
VOLUME No. V.

SUPREME GRAND LODGE OF AMORC
Printing and Publishing Department
San Jose, California

IMPRIMATUR

PROFUNDIS, F. R. C., XIII

First Edition
July, 1925

Second Edition
February, 1929

Third Edition
August, 1929

Fourth Edition
September, 1929

Fifth Edition
December, 1930

Sixth Edition
December, 1932

Seventh Edition
May, 1934

Eighth Edition
September, 1936

Ninth Edition
September, 1938

Tenth Edition
December, 1940

Eleventh Edition
July, 1943

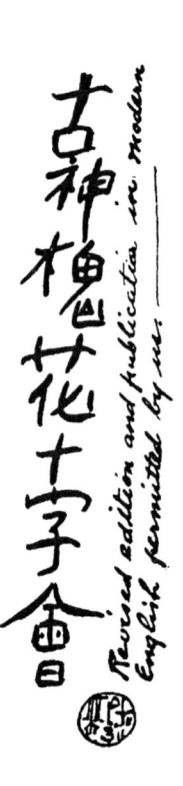

Contents

▽

BOOK FOUR

Consanguinity; Or Natural Relations

BOOK FIVE

Providence: Or the Accidental Differences of Men

BOOK SIX

The Social Duties

BOOK SEVEN

PART TWO

BOOK EIGHT

MAN CONSIDERED IN GENERAL

BOOK NINE

MAN CONSIDERED IN REGARD TO HIS INFIRMITIES, AND THEIR EFFECTS

BOOK TEN

OF THE AFFECTATIONS OF MAN, WHICH ARE HURTFUL TO HIMSELF AND OTHERS

BOOK ELEVEN

Of the Advantages Man May Acquire Over His Fellow Creatures

BOOK TWELVE

The Manifestations of Karma

Preface

THE STRANGE STORY OF THIS BOOK

▽

The original preface and introduction to the matter in this book gives us the following strange and interesting story of the origin, discovery, and translation of this rare mystical work.

An English gentleman of high associations went to China in the years between 1740 and 1750. There are indications that he was commissioned by the Earl of Derby and others interested in historical and geographical explorations to gather special data and information not generally known at that time. The English gentleman, who was evidently a brilliant scholar, linguist, and scientist, succeeded in making the acquaintance of a number of high officials. He sent weekly letters of great length in the form of reports to the groups of men in England who had commissioned him and, on a number of occasions, addressed some very long letters to the Earl of Derby personally. Many of these letters have become monuments of historical and geographical interest and some of these were published in book form in the year 1760, according to the records in London.

Most important of the letters sent to the Earl of Derby, however, was one which would have been sufficient preface for this work if the reader thereof had been familiar with all that preceded that letter. This particular letter addressed to the Earl of Derby is dated "Peking, May 12, 1749." In this letter the English gentleman says that he has just learned of and come in contact with a most interesting incident. Part of the letter is as follows:

"To the Earl ——,
"(London, England.)

"Peking, May 12, 1749.

"In the last letters which I had the honour of writing to your Lordship, dated December 23, 1748, I think I concluded all I had to say in regard to the topography and natural history of this great empire. I purposed in this, and some succeeding notes, to have set down such observations as I have been able to make on the laws, government, religion, and manners of the people. But a remarkable occurrence has happened lately, which ingrosses the conversation of the literati here and may hereafter afford matter of speculation to the learned in Europe. . . .

"Adjoining China on the West, is the large country of Tibet, called by some Barantola. In a province of this country, named Lasa, resides the Grand Lama, or High Priest, who is reverenced, and even adored as a god, by most of the neighboring nations. The high opinion which is entertained of this sacred character induces prodigious numbers of religious people to resort to Lasa, to pay their homage to him, and to give him presents, in order to receive his blessings. His residence is in a most magnificent pagod, or temple, built on the top of the mountain Poutala. The foot of this mountain, and even the whole district of Lasa, is inhabited by an incredible number of Lamas, of different ranks and Orders; several of whom have very great pagods erected to their honor. . . . The whole country, like Italy, abounds with priests; and they entirely subsist on the great numbers of rich presents which are sent them from the utmost extent of Tartary, from the empire of the Indies. When the Grand Lama receives the adoration of the people, he is raised on a magnificent altar, and sits cross-legged upon a splendid cushion. His worshippers prostrate themselves before him in the humblest and most abject manner; but he returns not the least sign of respect, nor ever speaks, even to the greatest princes. He only lays his hand upon their heads and they are fully persuaded that they receive from thence a full forgiveness of all their sins. They are likewise so extravagant as to believe that he knows all things, even the secrets of the heart; and his particular disciples being a *select number of about two hundred* of the most eminent Lamas, have the address to make the people believe he is immortal; and that whenever he appears to die, he only changes his abode and animates a new body.

"The learned in China have long been of opinion that, *in the archives of this grand temple,* some very ancient books have for many ages been *concealed;* and the present Emperor, who is very curious in searching after the writings of antiquity, became at length so fully *convinced* of the probability of this opinion, that he determined to try whether any discovery of this sort could be made. To this end, his first care was to find out a person emi-nently skillful in the ancient languages and characters. He at length pitched upon one of the Hanlins, or Doctors of the first Order, whose name was Cao-Tsou, a man about fifty years of age, of a grave and noble aspect of great eloquence, and who, by an accident friendship with a certain learned Lama, who had resided years at Peking, was become entirely master of the lan-guage which the Lamas of Tibet used among themselves.

"With these qualifications he set forward on his journey; and, to give his commission the greater weight, the *Emperor honoured him with the title of Cosao,* or Prime Minister. To which he added a most magnificent equipage and attendance, *with presents for the Grand Lama,* and the other principal Lamas, of an im-mense value! also a letter written with his own hand in the following terms."

(Herewith follows the letter which the Emperor of China in 1747 sent to the Grand Lama in Tibet, now known as the Dalai Lama, whose seat of government is still at Lasa, now spelled Lhasa. One can easily visualize the scene of the messenger or Prime Minister from the Emperor's court arriving at Lhasa. One naturally recalls the visit of the Queen of Sheba to King Solomon with her many slaves carrying hundreds of precious gifts. Just what gifts the Emperor of China could send to the rich and mighty Grand Lama that would interest him, is hard to conceive, because the Grand Lama was surrounded with such wealth and such luxuries as all parts of the world could provide. However, the letter addressed to the Grand Lama is interesting and is published herewith as taken from the official records.)

"To the Great Representative of God.
"(The Grand Lama at Lasa.)
"Most High, Most Holy,
"and Worthy to be adored!

"We the emperor of China, Sovereign of all the Sovereigns of the earth, in the person of this our Most respected Prime Minister Cao-Tsou, with all reverence and humility, prostrate ourself be-neath thy sacred feet, and implore for ourself, our friends, and our empire, thy most powerful and gracious benediction.

"Having a strong desire to search into the records of antiquity to learn and retrieve the *wisdom of the ages* that are past; and being well informed, that, in the sacred *repositories* of thy most ancient and venerable hierarchy, there are some valuable books, which, from their great antiquity are become to the generality, even of the learned, almost wholly unintelligible; in order, as far as in us lies, to prevent their being totally lost, we have thought proper to *authorize and employ our* Most Learned and respected Minister Cao-Tsou in this our present embassy to thy Sublime Holiness. The business of which, is to desire, that he may be permitted to read and examine the said writings; we expecting from his great and uncommon skill in the ancient languages, that he will be able to *interpret whatever may be found,* though of the highest and *most obscure antiquity.* And we have commanded him to throw himself at thy feet, with such testimonials of our respect as we trust will procure him the admittance we desire."

(Signed by the Emperor of China.)

"I will not detain your Lordship with any particular of his journey, though he hath published a large account of it, abounding with many surprising relations. . . . Let it suffice at present, that when he arrived in these sacred territories, the magnificence of his appearance, and the richness of his presents, failed not to gain him a ready admission. *He had apartments appointed him in the sacred college, and was assisted* in his inquiries by one of the most learned Lamas. He continued there near *six months; during which he had the satisfaction* of finding *many valuable pieces of antiquity;* from some of which he hath made very curious extracts. . . .

"But the most ancient piece he hath discovered and which none of the Lamas for many ages had been able to interpret or understand, is a complete system of mystical instruction, written in the language and character of the ancient Gymnosophists or Bramins. This piece he wholly translated, though, as he himself confesses, with an utter incapacity of reaching, in the Chinese language, the strength and sublimity of the original. The judgments and opinions of the Bonzess, and the learned Doctors, are very much divided concerning it. Those who admire it the most highly, are very fond of *attributing it to Confucius,* their own great philosopher. . . . Some will have it to be the institute of Lao-Kiun, of the sect Tao-ssee. . . . There are others who from some particular marks and sentiments which they find in it, suppose it to be written by the Bramin, Dandamis, whose famous letter to Alexander the Great is recorded by the European writers. With these Cao-Tsou himself seems most inclined to agree; at least so far as to think, that it is really the work of some ancient Bramin; being fully persuaded from the spirit with which it is written, that it is no translation. . . .

"But whoever was the writer of it, the great noise which it makes in this city, and all over the empire, the eagerness with which it is read by all kinds of people, *and the high ecomiums which are given to it by some, at length determined me to attempt a translation of it into English;* especially as I was persuaded it would be an agreeable present to your Lordship. One thing, however, it may perhaps be necessary to apologize for, at least to give some account of; that is, the style and manner in which I have translated it. I can assure your Lordship that when I first sat down to the work, I had not the least intention of doing it this way; but the sublime manner of thinking which appeared on the shortness of the sentences, naturally led me into this kind of style.

"Such as it is, if it affords your Lordship any instruction, I shall think myself extremely happy; and in my next will resume my account of this people and their empire."

"I am, etc."

(Signed by an eminent English scholar.)

The privilege of translating the ancient manuscript was granted by the Grand Lama to the Prime Minister, who spent his six months' time in the sacred college translating this and other manuscripts which will probably come to light within this year. Many of the learned teachers and High Initiates assisted the Prime Minister and when the task was finished the translated manuscript was brought to the Emperor of China by the Prime Minister. Here, the English gentleman and his associates on the commission examined it, and with the permission of the Emperor of China and the linguists of the court, another translation was made of it in English, solely for the purpose of delivering the English copy to the Earl of Derby, as explained in the letter to the Earl reproduced above.

So remarkable was this translation and so unusual the doctrines and teachings contained therein, that the Earl of Derby authorized or permitted a reproduction of the translation in English to a limited number. These copies were well-bound and preserved and were finally distributed to the chief officers or executives of the several secret, mystic organizations then existing in Europe.

One of these copies has been preserved in the archives of one of these Brotherhoods ever since and was used as the foundation for its high and profound teachings. The chief officer of this Brotherhood realized recently that the legibility of the copy could not be preserved for more than a few years, because the old hand-made paper was becoming very yellow and crumbling to dust. Believing that there were hundreds of sincere students of the true doctrines of Tibet who might wish to study this rare work, he finally granted official permission to the present publishers to reproduce the book in the modern form without any fee or royalty payment to himself as owner of the work, provided that it was reproduced in its entirety and without changes or modifications in grammar that would alter the true meaning of any sentence or thought.

This is how the rare work came into the hands of the present publishers and appears now in its modern form.

ITS AUTHORSHIP

The reader will note in the letter from the English gentleman to the Earl of Derby that there is some speculation as to the author of the original manuscript. The Grand Lama and his associates claimed that the manuscript had been in their possession and used by them as a foundation for their teachings since 731 A. D. They meant that records indicated its existence at that time, but it may have been in the possession of some of their Adepts and Masters outside of Tibet for many years before that date.

It was natural for those in Tibet to attribute the manuscript to one of their great writers, such as Confucius or Lao-Tse, but in the light of modern research, and especially in the light of revelations made by the excavations in Egypt and Jerusalem within the past hundred years, and since 1749, when the Tibetan copy was translated into English, we can plainly see that the original manuscript was not written by Confucius or any one of his time, or nation, or beliefs. For example, a native of Tibet, or mountainous inner Asia, would not have been familiar with rocks on the seashore, and dashing waves (¶ 1, p. 9), nor mention such creatures as the crocodile which are found in Egypt rather than in Tibet.

There is every indication throughout the work as it appears on the following pages that most of it was written by Amenhotep IV, Pharaoh of Egypt, during the years 1360 to 1350 B. C., or thereafter, or by some of his successors in the great school of mysticism which he founded in Egypt.

Reference to any encyclopedia will reveal the fact that this Pharaoh upset the priesthood teachings and idol worship of Egypt by the establishment of monotheistic, mystical religion, and every authority on the history of religions points to him as the first man in the civilized world to proclaim the belief in one God; and he has been rightfully called "the greatest modernist of all times." He established a cult, or Secret Brotherhood, based upon this mystical religion, in the city which he founded and named Akhetaton.

Recent translations of the writings discovered on the walls and columns in his mystical temple in Egypt show, for instance, that he was the author of those beautiful passages which are incorporated in the Christian Bible as the hundred and fourth Psalm, and many sacred writings of the East have been very definitely traced to his school and Brotherhood.

Copies of the teachings and doctrines used in Egypt at that time undoubtedly reached Jerusalem and other parts of the world through the exodus of the Jews, and many proofs have been found to show that the high mystical teachings of this Pharaoh of Egypt and his followers were the foundation of such cults and schools as the Essenes to which the Master Jesus belonged, and which later evolved into a fraternity known as the "Brethren of the Rose Cross" or the *Rosicrucians*, referred to by Lord Bulwer-Lytton in his book "Zanoni" and by many others who have given time to such research, including Sir Francis Bacon, who at one time was chief executive of the Order of the Rosicrucians throughout continental Europe.

The probability of this authorship of the following doctrines makes this work one of the most important contributions to sacred literature and one of the most interesting teachings that has come to light in the past few centuries. Reproduced herewith, is the official warrant and privilege for the production of this book in modern form by the secret organization, whose chief executive possesses the only complete composite copy now known to exist.

The reader's attention is called to the translator's comments on the terms and phrases used in this work, appearing at the close of the last Chapter.

The publishers wish to permanently express their thanks and appreciation to Mr. and Mrs. J. B. C. of Vancouver, Canada, for their valuable help in the preparation of this book.

THE PUBLISHERS.

San Francisco, California, U. S. A.
May twentieth, nineteen hundred and twenty-five.

▽   ▽   ▽

Preliminary Instructions

∇.

BOW down your heads unto the dust, O ye inhabitants of earth! be silent and receive with reverence these instructions from on high.

Wherever the sun doth shine, wheresoever the wind doth blow, wheresoever there is an ear to hear, and a mind to conceive; there let the precepts of life be made known, let the maxims of truth be honoured and obeyed.

All things proceed from God. His power is unbounded. His wisdom is for eternity, and his goodness endureth forever.

He sitteth on His throne in the centre of the universe and the breath of His mouth giveth life to the world.

He toucheth the stars with His fingers, and they run their course rejoicing.

On the wings of the mind He walketh abroad, and performeth His will through all the regions of unlimited space.

Order and grace, and beauty spring from His hand.

The voice of wisdom speaketh in all His works; but the mortal understanding comprehendeth it not.

The shadows of mortal knowledge passeth over the brain of man as a dream; he seeth as in the dark; he reasoneth, and is deceived.

But the wisdom of God is as the Light of Heaven; it requireth not reason; His mind is the foundation of truth.

Justice and mercy wait before His throne; benevolence and love enlighten His countenance forever.

Who is like unto God in glory? Who in power shall contend with the Almighty? Hath He any equal in wisdom? Can any in goodness be compared unto Him? There is none other before Him!

He it is, O man, who hath created thee; thy present station on earth was fixed by His laws; the powers of thy mind are the gifts of His Goodness, the wonders of thy frame are the work of His hand; thy Soul is His Soul; thy consciousness His consciousness.

Hear then His Voice, for it is gracious; and he that obeyeth shall establish his mind in Peace Profound; and bring everlasting growth to the Soul that resideth within his body, state after state, on this earth.

Therefore, with these instructions,

Unto Thee I Grant
the Economy of Life,
Thy Master

▽   ▽   ▽

𝕭𝖔𝖔𝖐 𝕺𝖓𝖊

▽

THE OBLIGATIONS THAT RELATE TO MAN, CONSIDERED AS AN INDIVIDUAL

CHAPTER I

Consideration

COMMUNE with thyself, O man! and consider wherefore thou wert made.

Contemplate thy powers, contemplate thy wants and thy connections; so shalt thou discover the duties of life, and be directed in all thy ways.

Proceed not to speak or to act before thou hast weighed thy words, and examine the tendency of every step thou shalt take; so shall disgrace fly far from thee, and in thy house shall shame be a stranger; repentance shall not visit thee, nor sorrow dwell upon thy cheek in this or many lives to come.

The thoughtless man bridleth not his tongue; he speaketh at random and is entangled in the foolishness of his own words.

As one runneth in haste, and leapeth over a fence, may fall into a pit on the other side, which he doth not see; so is the man that plungeth suddenly into any action before he hath considered the consequences thereof, and the compensation which The Law will exact.

Hearken therefore unto the voice of Consideration; her words are the words of wisdom, and her paths shall lead thee to safety and truth.

[3]

CHAPTER II

Modesty

Who art thou, O man! that presumest on thine own wisdom? or why dost thou vaunt thyself on thine own acquirements?

The first step towards being wise, is to know that thou art born mortally ignorant; and if thou wouldst not be esteemed foolish in the judgment of others, cast off the folly of being wise in thine own mortality.

As a plain garment best adorneth a beautiful woman, so a decent behaviour is the greatest ornament of inner wisdom.

The speech of a modest man giveth lustre to truth, and the diffidence of his words absolveth his error.

He relieth not on his mortal wisdom; he weigheth the counsel of a friend, and receiveth the benefit thereof.

He turneth away his ear from his own praise, and believeth it not; he is the last in discovering his own perfections.

Yet, as a veil addeth to beauty, so are his virtues set off by the shade which his modesty casteth upon them.

But behold the vain man, and observe the arrogant; he clotheth himself in rich attire, he walketh in the public street, he casteth around his eyes, and courteth observation.

He tosseth up his head, and overlooketh the poor; he treateth his inferiors with insolence, his superiors in return look down on his pride and folly with laughter.

He despiseth the judgment of others; he relieth on his own opinion, and is confounded.

He is puffed up with the vanity of his imagination; his delight is to hear, and to speak of himself all the day long.

He swalloweth with greediness his own praise, and the flatterer in return eateth him up.

CHAPTER III

Application

Since the days that are past are gone forever, and those that are to come may not come to thee in thy present state of being, it behooveth thee, O man! to employ the present state, without regretting the loss of that which is past, or too much depending on that which is to come; for of thy next state thou canst not know except as thy actions now ordain them.

This instant is thine; the next is in the womb of futurity, and thou knowest not what it may bring forth; maturity of the unborn is in the keeping of the Law.

Each future state is that thou has created in the present.

Whatsoever thou resolvest to do, do it quickly. Defer not till the evening what the morning may accomplish.

Idleness is the parent of want and pain; but the labour of Goodness bringeth forth pleasure.

The hand of diligence defeateth want; prosperity and success are the industrious man's attendants.

Who is he that hath acquired wealth, that hath risen to power, that hath clothed himself with honour, that is spoken of in the city with praise and that standeth before the king in his counsel? Even he that hath shut out idleness from his house, and hath said, "Sloth thou art mine enemy."

He riseth up early, and lieth down late; he exerciseth his mind with contemplation, and his body with action, and preserveth the health of both.

The slothful man is a burden to himself, his hours hang heavy on his head; he loitereth about, and knoweth not what he would do.

His days pass away like the shadow of a cloud, and he leaveth behind him no sign for remembrance.

His body is diseased for want of exercise, he wisheth for action, but hath not power to move; his mind is in darkness; his thoughts are confused; he longeth for knowledge, but hath no application.

He would eat of the almond, but hateth the trouble of breaking its shell.

His house is in disorder, his servants are wasteful and riotous, and he runneth on toward ruin; he seeth it with his eyes, he heareth it with his ears, he shaketh his head, and wisheth, but hath no resolution; till ruin cometh upon him like a whirlwind, and shame and repentance descend with him to the grave. Yet shall come a day from the Heavens thy Soul returneth and shall gather up the dust and animate it.

Chapter IV

Emulation

If thy heart thirsteth for honour, if thy ear hath any pleasure in the voice of praise, raise thy mortal self from the dust whereof thou art made; and exalt thy aim to something that is praiseworthy.

The oak that now spreadeth its branches toward the heavens was once but an acorn in the bowels of the earth. Endeavour to be first in thy calling, whatever it may be; neither let anyone go before thee in well-doing; nevertheless, do not envy the merits of another but improve thine own talents.

Scorn also to depress thy competitor by any dishonest or unworthy method; strive to raise thyself above him only by excelling him; so shall thy contest for superiority be crowned with honour, if not with success.

By virtuous emulation the spirit of man is exalted within him; he panteth after fame, and rejoiceth as a racer to run his course.

He riseth like the palm-tree in spite of oppression; and, as an eagle in the firmament of heaven, he soareth aloft, and fixeth his eye upon the glories of the sun.

The examples of eminent men are in his vision by night; and his delight is to follow them all the day long.

He formeth great designs, he rejoiceth in the execution thereof, and his name goes forth to the ends of the world.

But the heart of the envious man is gall and bitterness; his tongue spitteth venom; the success of his neighbour breaketh his rest.

He sitteth in his cell repining; and the good that happened to another, is to him an evil.

Hatred and malice feed upon his heart, and there is no rest in him.

He feeleth in his own breast no love of goodness, and therefore believeth his neighbour is like unto himself.

He endeavoureth to depreciate those that excel him, and putteth an evil interpretation on all their doings.

He lieth on the watch and meditateth mischief; but the detestation of man pursueth him, he is crushed as a spider in his own web.

Chapter V

Prudence

Hear the words of prudence, give heed unto her counsels, and store them in thine heart; her maxims are universal, and all the virtues lean upon her; she is the guide and the mistress of human life.

Put a bridle on thy tongue; set a guard before thy lips, lest the words of thine own mouth destroy thy peace.

Let him that scoffeth at the lame, take care he halt not himself; whosoever speaketh, shall hear his own words with bitterness of heart.

Of much speaking cometh repentance, but in silence is safety.

A talkative man is a nuisance to society, the ear is sick of his babbling, the torrent of his words overwhelming conversation.

Boast not of thyself, for it shall bring contempt upon thee; neither deride another, for it is dangerous.

A bitter jest is the poison of friendship, and he that cannot restrain his tongue, shall have trouble.

Furnish thyself with the proper accommodations belonging to thy condition; yet spend not to the utmost of what thou canst afford, that the providence of thy youth may be a comfort in thine old age.

Let thine own business engage thy attention; leave the care of the state to the governors thereof.

Let not thy recreations be expensive lest the pain of purchasing them exceed the pleasure thou hast in their enjoyment.

Neither let prosperity put out the eyes of circumstances, nor abundance cut off the hands of frugality; he that too much indulgeth in the superfluities of life, shall live to lament the want of its necessaries.

From the experience of others do thou learn wisdom; and from their feelings correct thine own faults.

Trust no man before thou hast tried him; yet mistrust not without reason; it is uncharitable.

But when thou hast proved a man to be honest, lock him up in thine heart as a treasure; regard him as a jewel of inestimable price.

Refuse the favours of a mercenary man; they will be a snare unto thee; thou shalt never be quit of his obligation.

Use not today what tomorrow may want; neither leave that to hazard which foresight may provide for, or care prevent.

Yet expect not even from prudence infallible success: for man knoweth not what the night may bring forth.

The fool is not always unfortunate, nor the wise man always successful; yet never had a fool a thorough enjoyment; never was a wise man wholly unhappy.

CHAPTER VI

Fortitude

Perils, and misfortunes, and want, and pain, and injury, are more or less the certain lot of every man that cometh into the world.

It behooveth thee, therefore, O child of calamity! early to fortify thy mind with courage and patience, that thou mayest support, with a becoming resolution, thy allotted portion of human evil.

As a camel beareth labour, and heat, and hunger, and thirst, through deserts of sand, and fainteth not; so the fortitude of man shall sustain him through all perils.

A noble spirit disdaineth the malice of fortune; his greatness of Soul is not to be cast down.

He hath not suffered his happiness to depend on her smiles, and therefore with her frowns he shall not be dismayed.

As a rock on the sea shore he standeth firm, and the dashing of the waves disturbeth him not.

He raiseth his head like a tower on a hill, and the arrows of fortune drop at his feet.

In the instant of danger, the courage of his heart sustaineth him; and the steadiness of his mind beareth him out.

He meeteth the evils of life as a man that goes forth unto battle and returneth with victory in his hand.

Under the pressure of misfortune his calmness alleviates their weight, and his constancy shall surmount them.

But the dastardly spirit of a timorous man betrayeth him to shame.

By shrinking under poverty, he stoopeth down to mean-ness; and by tamely bearing insults he inviteth insults.

As a reed is shaken with the breath of the air, so the shadow of evil maketh him tremble.

In the hour of danger, he is embarrassed and con-founded; in the day of misfortune he sinketh and despair overwhelmeth his Soul.

Chapter VII

Contentment

Forget not, O man! that thy present station on earth is appointed by the wisdom of the Eternal; who knoweth thy heart, who seeth the vanity of all thy wishes, and who often, in mercy, denieth thy requests.

Yet for all reasonable desires, for all honest endeavors, his benevolence has established, in the nature of things, a probability of success.

The uneasiness thou feelest, the misfortunes thou be-waileth, behold the root from whence they spring, even thine own folly, thine own pride, thine own distem-pered fancy.

Murmur not therefore at the dispensation of God, but correct thine own heart: neither say within thyself, if I had wealth, or power, or leisure, I should be happy; for know, they all of them bring to their several possessors their peculiar inconveniences.

The poor man seeth not the vexations and anxieties of the rich, he feeleth not the difficulties and perplexities of power, neither knoweth he the wearisomeness of leisure; and threfore it is that he repineth at his own lot.

But envy not the appearance of happiness in any man, for thou knowest not his secret griefs.

To be satisfied with a little, is the greatest wisdom; and he that increaseth his riches, increaseth his cares; but a contented mind is a hidden treasure, and trouble findeth it not.

Yet if thou sufferest not the allurement of fortune to rob thee of justice, or temperance, or charity, or modesty, even riches themselves shall not make thee unhappy.

But hence shalt thou learn, that the cup of felicity, pure and unmixed, is by no means a draught for mortal man.

Goodness is the race which God hath set him to run, and happiness the goal; which none can arrive at till he hath finished his course, and receiveth his crown in the mansions of eternity.

CHAPTER VIII

Temperance

The nearest approach thou canst make to happiness is to enjoy from Heaven understanding and health.

These blessings if thou possessest and wouldst preserve to old age, avoid the allurements of Voluptuousness, and fly from temptations.

When she spreadeth her delicacies on the board, when her wine sparkleth in the cup, when she smiles upon thee, and persuadeth thee to be joyful and happy; then is the hour of danger, and let Reason stand firmly on her guard.

For if thou hearkenest unto the words of the Adversary, thou art deceived and betrayed.

The joy which she promiseth changeth to madness, and her enjoyments lead on to diseases and death.

Look round her board, cast thine eyes upon her guests and observe those who have been allured by her smiles, who have listened to her temptations.

Are they not meagre? Are they not sickly? Are they not spiritless?

Their short hours of jollity and riot are followed by tedious days of pain and dejection. She hath debauched and palled their appetites, and they have now no relish for her nicest dainties; her votaries are become her victims; the just and natural consequences which God hath ordained, in the constitution of things, for the punishment of those who abuse His gifts.

But who is she that with graceful steps, and with a lively air trips over yonder plain?

The rose blusheth on her cheeks, the sweetness of the morning breatheth from her lips; joy, tempered with innocence and modesty, sparkleth in her eyes and from the cheerfulness of her heart she singeth as she walks.

Her name is Health: she is the daughter of Exercise, who begot her on Temperance; their sons inhabit the mountains that stretch over the northern regions of San Ton Hoe.

They are brave, active, and lively and partake of all the beauties and virtues of their sister.

Vigour strengtheneth their nerves, strength dwelleth in their bones, and labour is their delight all the day long.

The employments of their father excite their appetites, and the repasts of their mother refresh them.

To combat the passions is their delight; to conquer evil habits, their glory.

Their pleasures are moderate, and therefore they endure; their repose is short, but sound and undisturbed.

Their blood is pure, their minds are serene, and the physician findeth not the way to their habitations.

But safety dwelleth not with the sons of men, neither is security found within their gates.

Behold them exposed to new dangers from without, while a traitor within lurketh to betray them.

Their health, their strength, their beauty, and activity, have raised desire in the bosom of lascivious Love.

She standeth in her bower, she courteth their regard, she spreadeth her temptations.

Her limbs are soft and delicate, her attire is loose and inviting, wantonness speaketh in her eyes, and on her bosom sits Temptation. She beckoneth them with her finger, she wooeth them with her looks, and by the smoothness of her tongue she endeavoureth to deceive.

Ah! fly from her allurements, stop thine ears to her enchanting words. If thou meetest the languishing of her eyes, if thou hearest the softness of her voice, if she casteth her arms about thee, she bindeth thee in chains for ever.

Shame followeth, and disease, and want, and care, and repentance.

Enfeebled by dalliance, with luxury pampered, and softened by sloth, strength shall foresake thy limbs, and health thy constitution. Thy days shall be few and those inglorious; thy griefs shall be many, yet meet with no compassion.

Book Two

▽

THE PASSIONS

CHAPTER I

Hope and Fear

PROMISES of Hope are sweeter than the rose in the bud, and far more flattering to expectation, but the threatenings of Fear are a cross upon which the rose is crucified.

Nevertheless, let no Hope allure, nor Fear deter thee from doing that which is right; so shalt thou be prepared to meet all events with an equal mind.

The terrors even of death are no terrors to the good; he that committeth no evil, hath nothing to fear.

In all thy undertakings, let a reasonable assurance animate they endeavors; if thou despairest of success, thou shalt not succeed.

Terrify not thy Soul with vain fears, neither let thy heart sink within thee from the phantoms of imagination.

From Fear proceedeth misfortune; but he that hopeth, helpeth himself.

As the ostrich when pursued hideth his head, but forgetteth his body; so the fears of a coward expose him to danger.

If thou believest a thing impossible, thy despondency shall make it so; but he that persevereth, shall overcome all difficulties.

A vain hope flattereth the heart of a fool; but he that is wise, pursueth it not.

In all thy desires, let reason go along with thee, and fix not thy hopes beyond the bounds of probability; so shall success attend thy undertakings, thy heart shall not be vexed with disappointment.

CHAPTER II

Joy and Grief

Let not thy mirth be so extravagant as to intoxicate thy mind, nor thy sorrow so heavy as to depress thy heart. This world affordeth no good so transporting, nor inflicteth any evil so severe as should raise thee far above, or sink thee much beneath, the balance of moderation.

Lo! yonder standeth the house of Joy. It is painted on the outside, and looketh gay; thou mayest know it from the continual noise of mirth and exultation that issueth from it.

The mistress standeth at the door, and calleth aloud to all that pass by; she singeth and shouteth, and laugheth without ceasing.

She inviteth them to go in and taste the pleasures of life, which she telleth them are nowhere to be found but beneath her roof.

But enter not thou into her gate without care; neither associate thyself with those who frequent her house, unduly and immorally.

They call themselves the sons of Joy, they laugh and seem delighted; but madness and folly are in all their doings.

They are linked with mischief hand in hand, and their steps lead down to evil. Dangers beset them round about, and the pit of destruction yawneth beneath their feet.

Look now on the other side; and behold, in that vale overshadowed with trees, and hid from the sight of men, the habitation of Sorrow.

Her bosom heaveth with sighs, her mouth is filled with lamentation, she delighteth to dwell on the subject of human misery.

She looketh on the common accidents of life, and weepeth, the weakness and wickedness of man is the theme of her lips.

All nature to her teemeth with evil, every object she seeth is tinged with the gloom of her own mind, and the voice of complaint saddeneth her dwelling day and night.

Come not near her cell; her breath is contagious; she will blast the fruits and wither the flowers that adorn and sweeten the garden of life.

In avoiding the house of Joy, let not thy feet betray thee to the borders of this dismal mansion; but pursue with care the middle path, which shall lead thee by a gentle ascent to the bower of Tranquility.

With her dwelleth peace, with her dwelleth safety and contentment. She is cheerful, but not gay; she is serious, but not grave; she vieweth the joys and the sorrows of life with an equal and steady eye.

From hence, as from an eminence, shalt thou behold the folly and the misery of those, who, led by the gaiety of their hearts, take up their abode with the companions of jollity and riotous mirth; or, infected by gloominess and melancholy, spend all their days in complaining of the woes and calamities of human life.

Thou shalt view them both with understanding, and the error of their ways shall keep thy feet from straying.

CHAPTER III

Anger

As the whirlwind in its fury teareth up trees, and deformeth the face of nature, or as an earthquake in its convulsions overturneth whole cities; so the rage of an angry man throweth mischief around him.

Danger and destruction wait on his hand.

But consider, and forget not thine own weakness; so shalt thou pardon the failings of others.

Indulge not thyself in the passion of Anger; it is whetting a sword to wound thine own breast, or murder thy friend.

If thou bearest slight provocations with patience, it shall be imputed unto thee for wisdom; and if thou wipest them from thy remembrance, thy heart shall not reproach thee.

Seest thou not that the angry man loseth his understanding? Whilst thou art yet in thy senses, let the wrath of another be a lesson to thyself.

Do nothing in a passion. Why wilt thou put to sea in the violence of a storm?

If it be difficult to rule thine anger, it is wise to prevent it; avoid therefore all occasions of falling into wrath, or guard thyself against them whenever they occur.

A fool is provoked with insolent speeches, but a wise man laugheth them to scorn.

Harbour, not revenge in thy breast; it will torment thy heart, and discolour its best inclinations.

Be always more ready to forgive, than to return an injury; he that watches for an opportunity of revenge, lieth in wait against himself, and draweth down mischief on his own head.

A mild answer to an angry man, like water cast upon the fire, abateth his heat; and from an enemy he shall become thy friend.

Consider how few things are worthy of anger, and thou wilt wonder that any but fools should be wroth.

In folly or weakness it always beginneth; but remember and be well assured, it seldom concludeth without repentance.

On the heels of folly treadeth shame; at the back of anger standeth remorse.

Chapter IV

Pity

As blossoms and flowers are strewed upon earth by the hand of spring, as the kindness of summer produceth in perfection the bounties of harvests; so the smiles of pity shed blessings on the children of misfortune.

He who pitieth another, recommendeth himself; but he who is without compassion, deserveth it not.

The butcher relenteth not at the bleating of the lamb; neither is the heart of the cruel moved with distress.

But the tears of the compassionate are sweeter than dew-drops, falling from roses on the bosom of spring.

Shut not thine ear therefore against the cries of the poor, neither harden thine heart against the calamities of the innocent.

When the fatherless call upon thee, when the widow's heart is sunk and she imploreth thy assistance with tears of sorrow; O pity her affliction and extend thy hand to those who have none to help them.

When thou seest the naked wanderer of the streets, shivering with cold and destitute of habitation; let bounty open thine heart, let the wings of charity shelter him from death, that thine own Soul may live.

Whilst the poor man groaneth on the bed of sickness, whilst the unfortunate languish in the horrors of a dungeon, or the hoary head of age lifts up a feeble eye to thee for pity; O how canst thou riot in superfluous enjoyments, regardless of their wants, unfeeling of their woes?

CHAPTER V

Desire and Love

Beware, young man, beware of the allurements of wantonness, and let not the harlot to tempt thee to excess in her delights.

The madness of desire shall defeat its own pursuits; from the blindness of its rage thou shalt rush upon destruction.

Therefore give not up thy heart to her sweet enticements, neither suffer thy heart to be enslaved by her enchanting delusions.

The fountain of health, which must supply the stream of pleasure, shall quickly be dried up, and every spring of joy shall be exhausted.

In the prime of thy life, old age shall overtake thee; thy sun shall decline in the morning of thy days.

But when virtue and modesty enlighten her charms, the lustre of a beautiful woman is brighter than the stars of heaven, and the influence of her power is in vain to resist.

The whiteness of her bosom transcendeth the lily; her smile is more delicious than a garden of roses.

The innocence of her eyes is like that of the turtle; simplicity and truth dwell in her heart.

The kisses of her mouth are sweeter than honey; the perfumes of Arabia breathe from her lips.

Shut not thy bosom to the tenderness of love; the purity of its flame shall enoble thine heart, and soften it to receive the fairest impressions.

Book Three

▽

WOMAN

GIVE ear, fair daughter of love, to the instructions of prudence, and let the precepts of truth sink deep in thy heart; so shall the charms of thy mind add lustre to the elegance of thy form: and thy beauty like the rose it resembles, shall retain its sweetness when its bloom is withered.

In the spring of thy youth, in the morning of thy days, when the eyes of men gaze on thee with delight, and nature whispereth in thine ear the meaning of their looks; ah; hear with caution their seducing words, guard well thy heart, nor listen to their soft persuasions.

Remember thou art man's reasonable companion, not the slave of his passions; the end of thy being is not merely to gratify his loose desire, but to assist him in the toils of life, to sooth him with thy tenderness, and recompense his care with soft endearments.

Who is she that winneth the heart of man, that subdueth him to love and reigneth in his breast?

Lo! yonder she walketh in maiden sweetness, with innocence in her mind, and modesty on her cheek.

Her hand seeketh employment, her foot delighteth not in gadding abroad.

She is clothed in neatness, she is fed with temperance; humility and meekness are as a crown of glory circling her head.

On her tongue dwelleth music, the sweetness of honey floweth from her lips.

Decency is in all her words, in her answers are mildness and truth.

Submission and obedience are the lessons of her life, and peace and happiness are her reward.

Before her steps walketh prudence, and virtue attendeth at her right hand.

Her eye speaketh softness and love; but discretion with a sceptre sitteth on her brow.

The tongue of the licentious is dumb in her presence, the awe of her virtue keepeth him silent.

When scandal is busy, and the fame of her neighbour is tossed from tongue to tongue; if charity and good-nature open not her mouth, the finger of silence resteth on her lip.

Her breast is the mansion of goodness, and therefore she suspecteth no evil in others.

Happy were the man that should make her his wife; happy the child that shall call her mother.

She presideth in the house, and there is peace; she commandeth with judgment, and is obeyed.

She riseth in the morning, she considereth her affairs, and appointeth to every one their proper business.

The care of her family is her whole delight, to that alone she applieth her study; and elegance with frugality is seen in her mansions.

The prudence of her management is an honour to her husband, and he heareth her praise with a secret delight.

She informeth the minds of her children with wisdom, she fashioneth their manners from the example of her own goodness.

The word of her mouth is the law of their youth, the motion of her eye commandeth their obedience.

She speaketh and her servants fly; she pointeth and the thing is done; for the law of love is in their hearts, and her kindness addeth wings to their feet.

In prosperity she is not puffed up, in adversity she healeth the wounds of fortune with patience.

The troubles of her husband are alleviated by her counsels and sweetened by her endearments; he putteth his heart in her bosom and receiveth comfort.

Happy is the man that hath made her his wife; happy the child that calleth her mother.

Book Four

▽

CONSANGUINITY; OR NATURAL RELATIONS

CHAPTER I

Husband

CCEPT unto thyself a wife, and obey the ordinance of God; take unto thyself a wife, and become a faithful member of society.

But examine with care and fix not suddenly. On thy present choice depends thy future happiness.

If much of her time is destroyed in dress and adornments; if she is enamoured with her own praise; if she laugheth much, and talketh loud; if her foot abideth not in her father's house, and her eyes with boldness rove on the faces of men: though her beauty were as the sun in the firmament of heaven, turn thy face from her charms, turn thy feet from her paths, and suffer not thy mind to be ensnared by the allurements of imagination.

But when thou findest sensibility of heart, joined with softness of manners, an accomplished mind, with a form agreeable to thy fancy: take her home to thy house; she is worthy to be thy friend, thy companion in life, the wife of thy bosom.

O cherish her, as a blessing sent thee from Heaven; let the kindness of thy behaviour endear thee to her heart.

She is the mistress of thy house; treat her therefore with respect, that thy servants may obey her.

Oppose not her inclination without cause; she is the partner of thy cares, make her also the companion of thy pleasures.

Reprove her faults with gentleness, exact not her obedience with rigour.

Trust thy secret in her breast; her counsels are sincere,
thou shalt not be deceived.

Be faithful to her bed; for she is the mother of thy
children.

When pain and sickness assault her, let thy tenderness
sooth her affliction; a look from thee of pity and love shall
alleviate her grief, or mitigate her pain and be of more
avail than ten physicians.

Consider the tenderness of her sex, the delicacy of her
frame; and be not severe to her weakness, but remember
thine own imperfections.

Chapter II

Father

Consider, thou who art a parent, the importance of
thy trust; the being thou hast produced it is thy duty to
support.

Upon thee also it depends, whether the child of thy
bosom shall be a blessing, or a curse to thyself, a useful
or worthless member of the community.

Prepare him early with instruction, and season his mind
with maxims of truth.

Watch the bent of his inclinations, set him right in his
youth, and let no evil habit gain strength with his years.

So shall he rise like a cedar on the mountain; his head
shall be seen above the trees of the forest.

A wicked son is a reproach to his father; but he that
doeth right, is an honour to his gray hairs.

The soil is thine own, let it not want cultivation, the
seed which thou sowest, that also shalt thou reap.

Teach him obedience, and he shall bless thee; teach him
modesty, and he shall not be ashamed.

Teach him gratitude, and he shall receive benefits; each
him charity, and he shall gain love.

Teach him temperance, and he shall have health; teach
him prudence, and fortune shall attend him.

Teach him justice and he shall be honoured by the world; teach him sincerity, and his own heart shall not reproach him.

Teach him diligence, and his wealth shall increase; teach him benevolence and his find shall be exalted.

Teach him science, and his life shall be useful; teach him religion, and his death shall be happy.

CHAPTER III

Son

From the creatures of God let man learn wisdom, and apply to himself the instruction they give.

Go to the desert, my son; observe the young stork of the wilderness, let him speak to thy heart; he beareth on his wings his aged sire, he lodgeth him in safety, and supplieth him with food.

The piety of a child is sweeter than the incense of Persia offered to the sun; yea, more delicious than odours wafted from a field of Arabian spices by the western gales.

Be grateful then to thy father, for he gave thee life; and to thy mother for she sustained thee.

Hear the words from his mouth, for they are spoken for thy good; give ear to his admonition, for it proceedeth from love.

He hath watched for thy welfare, he hath toiled for thy ease; do honour therefore to his age, and let not his gray hairs be treated with irreverence.

Forget not thy helpless infancy, nor the forwardness of thy youth, and indulge the infirmities of thy aged parents; assist and support them in the decline of life.

So shall their hoary heads go down to the grave in peace; and thine own children, in reverence of thy example, shall repay thy piety with filial love.

CHAPTER IV

Brothers

Ye are the children of one father, provided for by his care; and the breast of one mother hath given you suck.

Let the bonds of affection, therefore, unite thee with thy brothers, that peace and happiness may dwell in thy father's house.

And when ye separate in the world, remember the relation that bindeth you to love and unity; and prefer not a stranger before thy own blood.

If thy brother is in adversity, assist him; if thy sister is in trouble forsake her not.

So shall the fortune of thy father contribute to the support of his whole race; and his care be continued to you all, in your love to each other.

Book Five

▽

PROVIDENCE; OR, THE ACCIDENTAL DIFFERENCES OF MEN

CHAPTER I

Wise and Ignorant

JOYS of the understanding are the treasures of God; and He appointeth to every one his portion in what measure seemed good unto Himself.

Hath He endued thee with wisdom? hath He enlightened thy mind with the knowledge of truth? Communicate it to the ignorant, for their instruction; communicate it to the wise, for thine own improvement.

True wisdom is less presuming than folly. The wise man doubteth often, and changeth his mind: the fool is obstinate, and doubteth not; he knoweth all things, but his own ignorance.

The pride of emptiness is an abomination; and much talk is the foolishness of folly; nevertheless, it is the part of wisdom, to bear with patience their impertinence, and to pity their absurdity.

Yet be not puffed up in thine own conceit, neither boast of superior understanding; the clearest human knowledge is but blindness and folly.

The wise man feeleth his imperfections and is humble; he laboureth in vain for his own approbation; but the fool peepeth in the shallow stream of his own mind, and is pleased with the pebbles which he seeth at the bottom: he bringeth them up, and sheweth them as pearls; and with the applause of his brethren, delighteth he himself.

He boasteth of attainments in things that are of no worth; but where it is a shame to be ignorant, there he hath no understanding.

Even in the paths of wisdom, he toileth after folly; and shame and disappointments are rewards of his labour.

But the wise man cultivates his mind with knowledge; the improvement of arts is his delight; and their utility to the public crowneth him with honour.

Nevertheless, the attainment of virtue he accounteth as the highest learning; and the science of happiness is the study of his life.

CHAPTER II

Rich and Poor

The man, to whom God hath given riches and blessed with a mind to employ them aright, is peculiarly favoured and highly distinguished.

He looketh on his wealth with pleasure, because it affordeth him the means to do good.

He protecteth the poor that are injured, he suffereth not the mighty to oppress the weak.

He seeketh out objects of compassion, he enquireth into their wants, he relieveth them with judgment and ostentation.

He assigneth and rewardeth merit; he encourageth ingenuity and liberally promoteth every useful design.

He carrieth on great works, his country is enriched, and the labourer is employed; he formeth new schemes, and the arts receive improvement.

He considereth the superfluities of his table as belonging to the poor of his neighbourhood, and he defraudeth them not.

The benevolence of his mind is not checked by his fortune; he rejoiceth therefore in riches, and his joy is blameless.

But woe unto him that heapeth up wealth in abundance, and rejoiceth alone in the possession thereof.

That grindeth the face of the poor, and considereth not the sweat of their brows.

He thriveth on oppression without feeling; the ruin of his brother disturbeth him not.

The tears of the orphan he drinketh as milk; the cries of the widow are music to his ear.

His heart is hardened with the love of wealth; no grief nor distress can make impression upon it.

But the curse of iniquity pursueth him; he liveth in continued fear; the anxiety of his mind, and the rapacious desires of his own Soul, take vengeance upon him, for the calamities he hath brought upon others.

O what are the miseries of poverty, in comparison with the gnawing of this man's heart!

Let the poor man comfort himself, yea, rejoice; for he hath many reasons.

He sitteth down to his morsel in peace, his table is not crowded with flatterers and devourers.

He is not embarrassed with a train of dependents, nor teased with the clamours of solicitation.

Debarred from the dainties of the rich he escapeth also their diseases.

The bread that he eateth, is it not sweet to his taste? The water he drinketh, is it not pleasant to his thirst? yea, far more delicious than the richest draughts of the luxurious.

His labour preserveth his health, and procureth him a repose, to which the down bed of sloth is a stranger.

He limiteth his desires with humility, and the calm of contentment is sweeter to his Soul, than all the acquirements of wealth and grandeur.

Let not the rich therefore presume on his riches, nor the poor in his poverty yield to despondence; for the providence of God dispenseth happiness to them both.

Chapter III

Masters and Servants

Repine not, O man, at the state of servitude: it is the appointment of God, and hath many advantages; it removeth thee from the cares and solicitudes of life.

The honour of a servant is his fidelity; his highest virtues are submission and obedience.

Be patient therefore under the reproofs of thy master; and when he rebuketh thee, answer not again: the silence of thy resignation shall not be forgotten.

Be studious in his interests, be diligent in his affairs, and faithful to the trust which he reposeth in thee.

Thy time and thy labour belong unto him; defraud him not thereof, for he payeth thee for them.

And thou, who art a master, be just to thy servant, if thou expectest from him fidelity; and reasonable in thy commands, if thou expectest a ready obedience.

The spirit of a man is in him; severity and rigour may create fear, but can never command his love.

Mix kindness with reproof and reason with authority; so shall thy admonitions take place in his heart, and his duty shall become his pleasure.

He shall serve thee faithfully from the motive of gratitude; he shall obey thee cheerfully from the principle of love; and fail not thou, in return to give diligence and fidelity their proper reward.

Chapter IV

Magistrates and Subjects

O Thou; the favourite of Heaven, whom the sons of men, thy equals, have agreed to raise to sovereign power, and set as a ruler over themselves; consider the ends and importance of their trust, far more than the dignity and height of thy station.

Thou art clothed in purple, and seated on a throne; the crown of majesty investeth thy temples, the sceptre of these ensigns given; nor meant for thine own, but the good of thy kingdom.

The glory of a king is the welfare of his people; his power and domain resteth on the hearts of his subjects.

The mind of a great prince is exalted with the grandeur of his situation; he resolveth high things, and searcheth for business worthy of his power.

He calleth together the wise men of his kingdom, he consulteth among them with freedom, and heareth the opinions of them all.

He looketh among his people with discernment, he discovereth the abilities of men, and employeth them according to their merits.

His magistrates are just, his ministers are wise and the favourite of his bosom deceiveth him not.

He smileth on the arts, and they flourish; the sciences improve beneath the culture of his hand.

With the learned and ingenious he delighteth himself, he kindleth in their breasts emulation, and the glory of his kingdom is exalted by their labours.

The spirit of the merchant who extendeth his commerce, the skill of the farmer who enricheth his lands, the ingenuity of the artist, the improvements of the scholar; all these he honoureth with his favour, or rewardeth with his bounty.

He planneth new colonies, he buildeth strong ships, he openeth rivers for convenience, he formeth harbours for safety; his people abound in riches, and the strength of his kingdom increaseth.

He frameth his statutes with equity and wisdom; his subjects enjoy the fruits of their labour in security; and their happiness consists in their observation of the law.

He foundeth his judgments on the principles of mercy; but, in the punishment of offenders, he is strict and impartial.

His ears are open to the complaints of his subjects: he restraineth the hand of their oppressors, and delivereth them from tyranny.

His people therefore look up to him as a father, with reverence and love; they consider him as the guardian of all they enjoy.

Their affection unto him begetteth in his breast a love of the public; the security of their happiness is the object of his care.

No murmurs against him arise in their heart; the machinations of his enemies endanger not his state.

His subjects are faithful, and firm in his cause; they stand in his defense as a wall of brass; the army of a tryant flieth before them as chaff before the wind.

Security and peace bless the dwellings of his people; and glory and strength encircle his throne for ever.

Book Six

▽

THE SOCIAL DUTIES

CHAPTER I

Benevolence

WHEN thou considerest thy wants, when thou beholdest thy imperfections, acknowledge His goodness, O son of humanity! who honoured thee with reason, enduced thee with speech, and placed thee in society to receive and confer reciprocal helps and mutual obligations

Thy food, thy clothing, thy conveniences of habitation; thy protection from the injuries, thy enjoyment of the comforts and the pleasures of life: all these thou owest to the assistance of others, and couldest not enjoy but in the bands of society.

It is thy duty therefore to be a friend to mankind, as it is thy interest that man should be friendly to thee.

As the rose breatheth sweetness from its own nature, so the heart of a benevolent man produceth good works.

He enjoyeth the ease and tranquility of his own breast, and rejoiceth in the happiness and prosperity of his neighbour.

He openeth not his ear unto slander; the faults and the failings of men give a pain in his heart.

His desire is to do good, and he searcheth out the occasions thereof; in removing the oppression of another, he relieveth himself.

From the largeness of his mind he comprehendeth in his wisdom the happiness of all men; and from the generosity of his heart he endeavoureth to promote it.

CHAPTER II

Justice

The peace of society dependeth on justice; the happiness of individuals on the safe enjoyment of all their possessions.

Keep the desires of thy heart, therefore, within the bounds of moderation: let the hand of justice lead them aright.

Cast not an evil eye on the goods of thy neighbour; let whatever is his property be sacred from thy touch.

Let no temptation allure thee, nor any provocation excite thee, to lift up thy hand to the hazard of his life.

Defame him not in his character; bear no false witness against him.

Corrupt not his servant to cheat or forsake him; and the wife of his bosom, O tempt not to sin!

It will be a grief to his heart which thou canst not relieve; an injury to his life, which no reparation can atone.

In thy dealings with men, be impartial and just, and do unto them as thou wouldst they should do unto thee.

Be faithful to thy trust, and deceive not the man who relieth upon thee; be asssured it is less evil in the sight of God to steal than to betray.

Oppress not the poor, and defraud not of his hire a labouring man.

When thou sellest for gain, hear the whisperings of conscience, and be satisfied with moderation; nor from the ignorance of the buyer make any advantage.

Pay the debts which thou owest; for he who gave thee credit, relied upon thy honour; and to withhold from him his due, is both mean and unjust.

Finally, O son of society! examine thy heart, call remembrance to thy aid; and if in any of these dealings thou findest thou hast transgressed, take sorrow and utmost of thy power.

CHAPTER III

Charity

Happy is the man who has sown in his breast the seeds of benevolence; the produce thereof shall be charity and love.

From the fountain of his heart shall rise rivers of goodness; and the streams shall overflow for the benefit of mankind.

He assisteth the poor in their trouble; he rejoiceth in furthering the prosperity of all men.

He censureth not his neighbour, he believeth not the tales of envy and malevolence; neither respecteth he their slanders.

He forgiveth the injuries of men, he wipeth them from his remembrance; revenge and malice have no place in his heart.

For evil he returneth not evil; he hateth not even his enemies, but requiteth their injustice with friendly admonition.

The griefs and anxieties of men excite his compassion; he endeavoureth to alleviate the weight of their misfortunes, and the pleasure of success rewardeth his labour.

He calmeth the fury, he healeth the quarrels of angry men, and preventeth the mischiefs of strife and animosity.

He promoteth in his neighbourhood peace and good-will, and his name is repeated with praise and benedictions.

CHAPTER IV

Gratitude

As the branches of a tree return their sap to the root, from whence it rose; as a river poureth its streams to the sea, whence its spring was supplied; so the heart of a grateful man delighteth in returning a benefit received.

He acknowledgeth his obligation with cheerfulness; he looketh on his benefactor with love and esteem.

And if to return it be not in his power, he nourisheth the memory of it in his breast with kindness, he forgeteth it not all the days of his life.

The hand of the generous man is like the clouds of heaven, which drop upon the earth, fruits, herbage and flowers; but the heart of the ungrateful is like a desert sand, which swalloweth with greediness the flowers that fall, and burieth them in its bosom and produceth nothing.

Envy not the benefactor; neither strive to conceal the benefit he hath conferred; for though to oblige is better than to be obligated, though the act of generosity commandeth admiration; yet the humility of gratiude toucheth the heart, and is amiable in the sight both of God and man.

But receive not a favour from the hand of the proud; to the selfish and avaricious have no obligation; the vanity of pride shall expose thee to shame, the greediness of avarice shall never be satisfied.

CHAPTER V

Sincerity

O thou who art enamoured with the beauties of Truth, and hast fixed thy heart on the simplicity of her charms, hold fast thy fidelity unto her, and forsake her not; the constancy of thy virtue shall crown thee with honour.

The tongue of the sincere is rooted in his heart; hypocrisy and deceit have no place in his words.

He blusheth at falsehood, and is confounded; but in speaking the truth he hath a steady eye.

He supporteth as a man the dignity of his character; to the arts of hypocrisy he scorneth to stoop.

He is confident with himself; he is never embarrassed; he hath courage enough for truth, but to lie he is afraid.

He is far above the meanness of dissimulation; the words of his mouth are the thoughts of his heart.

Yet with prudence and caution he openeth his lips; he studieth what is right, and speaketh with discretion.

He adviseth with friendship; he reproveth with freedom; and whatsoever he promiseth, shall surely be performed.

But the heart of the hypocrite is hid in his breast; he masketh his words in the semblance of truth, while the business of his life is only to deceive.

He laugheth in sorrow, he weepeth in joy; and the words of his mouth have no interpretation.

He worketh in the dark as a mole, and fancieth he is safe; but he blundereth into light, and is betrayed and exposed, with his dirt on his head.

He passeth his days in perpetual constraint; his tongue and his heart are for ever at variance.

He laboureth for the character of a righteous man; and huggeth himself in the thoughts of his cunning.

O fool, fool! the pains which thou takest to hide what thou art, are far more than would make thee what thou wouldst seem, and the children of wisdom shall mock at thy cunning when in the midst of security, thy disguise is stripped off, and the finger of derision shall point thee to scorn.

▽ ▽ ▽

Book Seven

▽

RELIGION

KNOW there is but one God, the author, the creator, the governor of the world; almighty, eternal, and incomprehensible.

The sun is not God, though His noblest image; he enlighteneth the world with his brightness, his warmth giveth life to the products of the earth; admire him as the creature, the instrument of God; but worship him not.

To the One who is supreme, most wise and beneficent, and to Him alone, belong worship, adoration, thanks-givings, and praise.

Who hath stretched forth the heaven with His hand, who hath described with His fingers the course of the stars.

Who setteth bounds of the ocean, that it cannot pass; and saith unto the stormy winds, Be still.

Who shaketh the earth, and the nations tremble; Who darteth His lightning, and the wicked are dismayed.

Who calleth forth worlds by the word of His mouth.

The providence of God is over all His work, He ruleth and directeth with infinite wisdom.

He hath instituted laws for the government of the world; He hath wonderfully varied them in all things, and each by his nature conformeth to His will.

In the depths of His mind He revolveth all knowledge; the secrets of futurity lie open before Him.

The thoughts of thy heart are naked to His view; He knoweth thy determinations before they are made.

With respect to His prescience, there is nothing contingent; with respect to His providence, there is nothing accidental.

Wonderful He is in all His ways; His counsels are inscrutable; the manner of His knowledge transcendeth thy conception.

Pay therefore to His wisdom all honour and veneration; and bow down thyself in humble and submissive obedience to His supreme direction.

God is gracious and beneficent; He hath created the world in mercy and love.

His goodness is conspicuous in all His works; He is the fountain of excellence, the centre of perfection.

The creatures of His hand declare His goodness, and all their enjoyments speak His praise; He clotheth them with beauty, He supporteth them with food, He preserveth them with pleasure from generation to generation.

If we lift up our eyes to the heavens, His glory shineth forth; if we cast them down upon the earth, it is full of His goodness; the hills and the valleys rejoice and sing; fields, rivers, and woods, resound His praise.

But thee, O man! He hath distinguished with peculiar favour; and exalted thy station above all creatures.

He hath endued thee with reason, to maintain thy dominance; He hath fitted thee with language, to improve thy society; and exalted thy mind with the powers of meditation, to conntemplate and adore His inimitable perfections.

And in the laws He hath ordained as the rule of thy life, so kindly hath He suited thy duty to thy nature, that obedience to His precepts is happiness to thy self.

O praise His goodness with songs of thanksgiving, and meditate in silence on the wonders of His love; let thy heart overflow with gratitude and acknowledgement, let the language of thy lips speak praise and adoration, let the actions of thy life show thy love to His law.

God is just and righteous, and will judge the earth with equity and truth.

Hath He established His laws in goodness and mercy, and shall He not punish the transgressors thereof?

O think not, bold man, because thy punishment is delayed, that the arm of God is weakened; neither flatter thyself with hopes that He winketh at thy doings.

His eye pierceth the secrets of every heart, and He remembereth them for ever; He respecteth neither the persons nor the stations of men.

The high and the low, the rich and the poor, the wise and the ignorant, when the Soul hath shaken off the cumbrous shackles of this mortal life, shall quickly receive from the Great Law of God, a just and everlasting compensation, according to their works.

Then shall the wicked learn and make compensation in course of time; but the heart of the righteous shall rejoice in His rewards.

O respect God, therefore, all the days of thy life, and walk in the paths which He hath opened before thee. Let prudence admonish thee, let temperance restrain, let justice guide thy hand, benevolence warm thy heart, and gratitude to heaven inspire thee with devotion. These shall give thee happiness in thy present state and future one and bring thee to the mansions of eternal felicity in the paradise of God.

This is the true Economy of Human Life.

End of Part One

▽ ▽ ▽

Part Two

▽

Book Eight

▽

MAN CONSIDERED IN THE GENERAL

CHAPTER I

Of the Human Frame and Structure

LOWLY and ignorant as thou art, O man! humble as thou oughtest to be, O child of the dust! wouldst thou raise thy thoughts to infinite wisdom? wouldst thou see omnipotence displayed before thee? Contemplate thine own frame.

Fearfully and wonderfully art thou made; praise therefore thy Creator with awe and rejoice before Him with reverence.

Wherefore of all creatures art thou only erect but that thou shouldst behold His works! wherefore art thou to behold, but that thou mayest admire them! wherefore to admire them, but that thou mayest adore their and thy Creator!

Wherefore is consciousness reposed in thee! and whence is it derived in thee!

It is not in flesh to think; it is not in bones to reason. The lion knoweth not that worms shall eat him; the ox perceiveth not that he is fed for slaughter.

Something is added to thee unlike to what thou seest; something animates thy clay higher than all that is the object of thy senses. Behold what is it?

Thy body remaineth perfect matter after IT is fled, therefore IT is no part of it; IT is immaterial, therefore IT is eternal; IT is free to act; therefore IT is accountable for its actions.

Knoweth the ass the use of food, because his teeth mow down the herbage? or standeth the crocodile erect, although his backbone is straight as thine?

God formed thee as He had formed these; after them all wert thou created; superiority and command were given thee over all, and of His own breath did He communicate to thee thy essence of consciousness.

Know thyself then the pride of His creation, the link uniting divinity and matter; behold a part of God Himself within thee; remember thine own dignity nor dare descend to evil or meanness.

Who planted terror in the tail of the serpent? who clothed the neck of the horse with thunder? even He who hath instructed thee to crush the one under thy feet, and to tame the other to thy purposes.

Chapter II

On the Use of the Senses

Vaunt not thy body, because it was first formed; nor thy mind because therein thy Soul resideth. Is not the master of the house more honourable than its walls?

The ground must be prepared before corn be planted; the potter must build his furnace before he can make his porcelain.

As the breath of Heaven sayeth unto the water of the deep: "This way shall thy billows roll, and no other; thus high and no higher, shall they raise their fury" so let Soul, O man, actuate and direct thy flesh; so let it repress thy wildness.

Thy Soul is the monarch of thy frame; suffer not its subjects to rebel against it.

Thy body is as the globe of the earth, thy bones the pillars that sustain it on its basis.

As the ocean giveth rise to springs, whose waters return again into its bosom through the rivers, so runneth thy life force from the heart outwards, and so returneth into its place again.

Do not both retain their course for ever? Behold, the same God ordained them.

Is not thy nose the channel to perfume? thy mouth the path to delicacies? Yet know thou, that perfumes long smelt become offensive, that delicacies destroy the appetite they flatter.

Are not thine eyes the outer sentinels that watch for thee? yet how often are they unable to distinguish truth from error?

Keep thy Soul in domination, teach thy spirit to be attentive to its work; so shall these ministers be always to thee conveyances of life.

Thine hand is it not a miracle, is there in the creation ought like unto it? Wherefore was it given thee, but that thou mightest stretch it out to the assistance of thy brother?

Why of all things living art thou alone made capable of blushing? the world shall read thy shame upon thy face; therefore do nothing shameful.

Fear and dismay, why rob they thy countenance of its ruddy splendour? avoid guilt, and thou shalt know that fear is beneath thee; that dismay is unmanly.

Wherefore to thee alone speak shadows in the visions of thy mind? Reverence them; for know that these are from on high.

Thou, man, alone canst speak. Wonder at thy glorious prerogative; and pay to Him who gave it thee a rational and welcome praise, teaching thy children wisdom, in-structing the offspring of thy loins in piety.

CHAPTER III

The Soul of Man, its Origins and Affections

The blessings, O man! of thy external part, are health, vigour, and proportion.

The greatest of these is health. What health is to the body, even that is honesty to the Soul.

That thou hast Soul, is of all knowledge the most certain, of all truths the most plain unto thee. Be meek, be grateful for it. Seek not to sense it perfectly, but commune with it.

Thinking, understanding, reasoning, willing, call not these Soul. They are its actions, but they are not its essence.

Search the Soul by its faculties, know it by its virtues. They are more in number than the hairs of thy head; the stars of Heaven are not to be counted with them.

Doth not the sun harden the clay? doth it not also soften the wax as it is one sun that worketh both, even so it is one Soul that willeth contrarities.

As the moon retaineth her nature, though darkness spread itself before her face as a curtain, so the Soul remaineth perfect even in the bosom of the fool.

She is immortal; she is unchangeable; she is one in all. Health calleth her forth to show her loveliness, and application anointeth her with the oil of wisdom.

She shall live after thee; think not she was born with thee. She was concreated for thy flesh, and formed with thy mind.

Justice could not give her to thee exalted by virtues, nor mercy deliver her to thee, deformed by vices. These must be thine, and thou must answer them with the outer consciousness.

Suppose not death can shield thee from compensation; think not corruption can hide thee from injury. He who formed thee of thou knowest not what, can He not raise thee from thou knowest not what again?

Perceiveth not the cock the hour of midnight? exalteth he not his voice, to tell thee it is morning? Knoweth not the dog the footsteps of his master? and flieth not the wounded goat unto the herb that healeth him? Yet, when these die, their Soul knoweth it not; thine alone surviveth with mind and consciousness.

Envy not to these their senses, because quicker than thine own, learn that the advantage lieth not in possessing good things, but in the knowing the use of them.

Hadst thou the ear of a stag, or were thine eyes as strong and piercing as the eagle's; didst thou equal the hound in smell, or could the ape resign to thee his taste, or the tortoise her feeling; yet, without reason, what would they avail thee? Perish not all these like their kindred?

Hath any one of them the gift of speech? Can they say unto thee therefore I did so?

The lips of the wise are as the doors of a cabinet; no sooner are they opened, but treasures are poured out before thee.

Like unto trees of gold arranged in beds of silver, are wise sentences uttered in due season.

Canst thou think too greatly of thy Soul? or can too much be said in its praise? it is the essence of Him who gave it.

Remember thou its dignity forever; forget not how great a talent is committed to thy charge.

Whatever may do good, may also do harm; beware that thou direct its course to virtue.

Think not that thou canst lose her in the crowd; suppose not thou canst bury her in thy closet. Action is her delight, and she will not be withheld from it.

Her motion is perpetual; her attempts are universal; her agility is not to be suppressed. Is it at the uttermost part of the earth she will have it; is it beyond the region of the stars? yet will her eye discover it.

Inquiry is her delight. As one who traverseth the burning sands in search of water, so is the Soul that thirsteth after knowledge.

As a sword in the hand of a madman, even so is the Soul of man who wanteth discretion.

The end of her search is truth; her means to discover it are reason and experience. But are not these weak, uncertain and fallacious? How then shall she attain unto it?

General opinion is no proof of truth; for the generality of men are ignorant.

Perception of thyself, the knowledge of Him who created thee, the sense of the worship thou owest unto Him, are not these plain before thy face? And, behold! what is there more that man needeth to know?

CHAPTER IV

Of the Period and Uses of Human Life

As the eye of morning to the lark, as the shade of evening to the owl, as the honey to the bee, or as the carcass to the vulture; even such is life unto the heart of man.

Though bright, it dazzleth not; though obscure it displeaseth not; though sweet it cloyeth not; though corrupt, it forbiddeth not; yet who is he that knoweth its true value?

Learn to esteem life as it ought; then art thou near the pinnacle of wisdom.

Think not with the fool, that nothing is more valuable; nor believe with the pretended wise, that thou oughtest to condemn it. Love it not for itself, but for the good it may be of to others.

Gold cannot buy it for thee, neither can mines of diamonds purchase back the moment thou hast now lost of it. Employ the succeeding one in virtue.

Say not, that it were best not to have been born; or, if born, that it had been best to die early; neither dare thou to ask of thy Creator, Where had been the evil had I not existed? Good is in thy power; the want of good is evil; and, if thy question be just, lo! it condemneth thee.

Would the fish swallow the bait if he knew the hook was hidden therein? would the lion enter the toils if he saw they were prepared for him? so neither were the Soul to perish with this clay, would man wish to live; neither would a merciful God have created him; know hence thou shalt live again and again.

As the bird inclosed in the cage before he seeth it, yet teareth not his flesh against its sides; so neither labour thou vainly to run from the state thou art in; but know it as allotted thee, and be content with it.

Though its ways are uneven, yet are they not at all painful. Accommodate thyself to all; and where there is least appearance of evil, suspect the greatest danger.

When thy bed is of straw, thou sleepeth in security; but when thou stretcheth thyself on roses, beware of the thorns!

A noble death is better than an evil life; strive to live therefore as long as thou oughtest, not as long as thou canst. While thy life is to others worth more than thy death, it is thy duty to preserve it.

Complain not with the fool of the shortness of thy time; remember that with thy days thy cares are shortened.

Take from the period of thy life the useless parts of it, and what remaineth? Take off the time of thine infancy, the second infancy of age; thy sleep, thy thoughtless hours, thy days of sickness, and, even at the fulness of years, how few seasons hast thou truly numbered?

He who gave thee life as a blessing, shortened it to make it more so. To what end would longer life have served thee? Wishest thou to have had an opportunity of more vices? As to the good, will not He who limited thy span, be satisfied with the fruits of it?

To what end, O child of sorrow! wouldst thou live longer? to breathe, to eat, to see the world? All this thou hast done already. Too frequent repetition is it not tiresome? or is it not superfluous?

Wouldst thou improve thy wisdom and thy virtue? Alas! what art thou to know? or who is it that shall teach thee? Badly thou employest the little thou hast, dare not therefore to complain that more is not given thee.

Repine not at the lack of knowledge; opportunity does not perish with thee in death. Be honest here, thou shalt be wise hereafter.

Say not unto the crow, Why number thou seven times the age of the lord? or to the fawn, Why are thine eyes to see my offspring to an hundred generations? Are these to be compared with thee in the abuse of life? are they riotous? are they cruel? are they ungrateful? Learn from them rather, that innocence of life and simplicity of manners, are the paths to a good old age.

Knowest thou to employ life better than these? then less of it may suffice thee.

Man who dares enslave the world, when he knows he can enjoy his tyranny but a moment, what would he not aim at, if he were immortal?

Enough hast thou of life, but thou regardest not; thou art not in want of it, O man! but thou art prodigal; thou throwest it lightly away, as if thou hadst more than enough!

Know that it is not abundance which maketh rich, but economy.

The wise continueth to live from his first period; the fool is always beginning.

Labor not after riches first, and think thou afterwards wilt enjoy them. He who neglecteth the present moment, throweth away all that he hath. As the arrow passeth through the heart, while the warrior knew not that it was coming; so shall his life be taken away before he knoweth that he hath it.

What then is life, that man should desire it? what breathing, that he should covet it?

Is it not a scene of delusion, a series of misadventures, a pursuit of evils linked on all sides together? In the beginning it is ignorance, pain is in its middle, and its end is sorrow.

As one wave pusheth on another, till both are involved in that behind them, even so succeedeth evil to evil in the life of man; the greater and the present swallow up the lesser and the past. Our terrors are real evils; our expectations look forward into improbabilities.

Fools dread as mortals, and desire as if immortal!

What part of life is it that we wish to remain with us? Is it youth? can we be in love with outrage, licentiousness, and termerity? Is it age? then are we fond of infirmities?

It is said gray hairs are revered, and in length of days is honour. Virtue can add reverence to the bloom of youth and without it, age plants more wrinkles in the Soul than on the forehead.

Is age respected because it hateth riot? What justice is in this, when it is not age despiseth pleasure, but pleasure despiseth age!

Be virtuous while thou art young, so shalt thine age be honoured.

Book Nine

∇

MAN CONSIDERED IN REGARD TO HIS INFIRMITIES, AND THEIR EFFECTS

CHAPTER I

Vanity

VANITY is powerful in the heart of man; intemperance swayeth it whither it will; despair ingrosseth much of it; and fear proclaimeth, "Behold, I sit unrivaled therein!" But vanity is beyond them all.

Weep not therefore at the calamities of the human state; rather laugh at its follies. In the hands of man addicted to vanity, life is but the shadow of a dream.

The hero, the most renowned of human characters, what is he but the bubble of this weakness? The public is unstable and ungrateful; why should the man of wisdom endanger himself for fools?

The man who neglecteth his present concerns, to resolve how he will behave when greater, feedeth himself with wind, while his bread is eaten by another.

Act as becometh thee in thy present station and in more exalted ones thy face shall not be ashamed.

What blindeth the eye, or what hideth the heart of a man from himself, like vanity? Lo! when thou seest not thyself, then others discover thee most plainly.

As the tulip is gaudy without smell, conspicuous without use; so is the man who setteth himself up on high and hath no merit.

The heart of the vain is troubled while it seemeth content; his cares are greater than his pleasures.

His solicitudes cannot rest with his bones; the grave is not deep enough to hide it; he extendeth his thoughts beyond his being; he bespeaketh praise to be paid when he is gone; but whoso promiseth it, deceiveth him.

As the man who engageth his wife to remain in widowhood, that she disturb not his Soul; so is he who expecteth that praise shall reach his ears beneath the earth, or cherish his heart in its shroud.

Do well while thou livest, but regard not what is said of it. Content thyself with deserving praise, and thy posterity shall rejoice in hearing it.

As the butterfly who seeth not her own colours, as the jessamine which feeleth not the scent it casteth around it; so is the man who appeareth gay, and bid-deth others to take notice of it.

To what purpose, saith he, is my vesture of gold? to what end are my tables filled with dainties, if no eye gaze upon them? if the world know it not? Give thy raiment to the naked, and thy food unto the hungry; so shalt thou be praised, and feel that thou deserveth it.

Why bestowest thou on every man the flattery of unmeaning words? Thou knowest when returned thee, thou regardest it not. He knoweth he lieth unto thee? yet he knoweth thou wilt thank him for it. Speak in sincerity and thou shalt hear with instruction.

The vain delighteth to speak of himself; but he seeth not that others like not to hear him.

If he has done anything worthy praise, if he possesseth that which is worthy admiration, his joy is to proclaim it, his pride is to hear it reported. The desire of such a man defeateth itself. Men say not, "Behold, he hath done it"; or, "See he possesseth it';; but, "Mark how proud he is of it!"

The heart of man cannot attend at once to many things. He who fixeth his Soul on show, loseth reality. He pursueth bubbles which break in their flight, while he treads to earth what would do him honour.

CHAPTER II

Inconstancy

Nature urgeth thee to inconstancy, O man! therefore guard thyself at all times against it.

Thou art from the womb of thy mother various and wavering; from the loins of thy father inheritedst thou instability: how then shalt thou be firm?

Those who gave thee a body, furnished it with weakness; but He who gave thee Soul, armed thee with resolution. Employ it, and thou art wise; be wise and thou art happy.

Let him who doth well, beware how he boasteth of it; for rarely is it of his own will.

Is it not the event of an impulse from without, born of uncertainty, enforced by accident, dependent on somewhat else? To these then, and to accidents, is due the praise.

Beware of irresolution in the intent of thy actions, beware of instability in the execution; so thalt thou triumph over two great failings of thy nature.

What reproacheth reason more than to act contrarities? What can suppress the tendnencies to these, but firmness of mind?

The inconstant feeleth that he changeth, but he knoweth not why; he seeth that he escapeth from himself but he perceiveth not how. Be thou incapable of change in that which is right, and men will rely upon thee.

Establish unto thyself principles of action; and see that thou ever act according to them.

First know that thy principles are just, and then be thou inflexible in the path of them.

So shall thy passion have no rule over thee; so shall thy constancy ensure unto thee the good thou possessest, and drive from the door misfortune. Anxiety and disappointment shall be strangers to thy gate.

Suspect not evil in any one, until thou seest it; when thou seest it, forget not to forgive.

How should his actions be right who hath no rule in life? Nothing can be just which proceedeth not from within.

The inconstant hath no peace in his Soul; neither can any be at ease whom he concerneth himself with.

His life is unequal; his motions are irregular; his reason changeth with the weather.

To-day he loveth thee, to-morrow thou art detested by him; and why? himself knoweth not wherefore he loved, or wherefore he now hateth.

To-day he is the tyrant, to-morrow thy servant is less humble; and why? he who is arrogant without power, will be servile where there is no subjection.

To-day he is profuse, to-morrow he grudgeth unto his mouth that which it should eat. Thus it is with him who knoweth not moderation.

Who shall say of the chameleon, He is black, when the moment after, the verdure of the grass overspreadeth him?

Who shall say of the innocent, He is joyful, when his next breath shall be spent in sighing?

What is life of such a man, but the phantom of a dream? In the morning he riseth happy, at noon he is on the rack; this hour he is a god, the next below a worm; one moment he laugheth, the next he weepeth; he now willeth, in an instant he willeth not, and in another he knoweth not whether he willeth or no.

Yet neither ease nor pain have fixed themselves on him; neither is he waxed greater, or become less; neither hath he had cause for laughter, nor reason for his sorrow; therefore shall none of them abide with him.

The happiness of the inconstant is as a place built on the surface of the land; the blowing of the wind carrieth away its foundation, what wonder then that it falleth?

But what exalted form is this, that hitherward directs its even, its uninterrupted course? whose foot is on the earth, whose head above the clouds? He is the constant being!

On his brow sitteth majesty; steadiness is in his port; and in his heart reigneth tranquility. . . .

Though obstacles appear in the way, he deigneth not to look down upon them; though heaven and earth oppose his passage, he proceedeth.

The mountains sink beneath his tread; the waters of the ocean are dried up and under the sole of his foot.

The tiger throweth herself across his way in vain; the spots of the leopard glow against him unregarded.

He marcheth through the imbattled legions; with his hands he putteth aside the terrors of death.

Storms roar against his shoulders, but are not able to shake them; the thunder bursteth over his head in vain; the lightening serveth but to show the glories of his countenance.

His name is resolution!

He cometh from the utmost part of the earth; he seeth happiness afar off before him; his eye discovereth her temple beyond the limits of the pole.

He walketh up to it, he entereth boldly, and he remaineth there for ever.

Establish thine heart, O man! in that which is right; and then know the greatest of human praise is to be immutable.

CHAPTER III

Weakness

Vain and inconstant if thou art, how canst thou but be weak? Is not inconstancy connected with frailty? can there be vanity without infirmity? Avoid the danger of the one, and thou shalt escape the mischief of the other.

Wherein art thou most weak? In that wherein thou seemeth most strong; in that wherein most thou gloriest; even in possessing the things which thou hast; in using the good that is about thee.

Are not thy wishes also frail? or knowest thou even what it is thou wouldst wish? When thou hast obtained what most thou soughtest after, behold it contenteth thee not.

Wherefore loseth the pleasure that is before thee its relish? and why appeareth that which is yet to come the sweeter? because thou are wearied with the goods of this, because thou knowest not the evil of that which is not with thee. Know that to be content, is to be happy.

Couldst thou choose for thyself; would thy Creator lay before thee all that thine heart could ask for; would happiness then remain with thee? or would joy dwell always in thy gates?

Alas! thy weakness forbiddeth it; thy infirmity declareth against it. Variety is to thee in the place of pleasure; but that which permanently delighteth, must be permanent.

When it is gone, thou repenteth the loss of it; though, while it was with thee, thou despisest it.

That which succeeded it, hath no more pleasure for thee; and thou afterwards quarrelest with thyself for preferring it; behold the only circumstance in which thou errest not!

Is there any thing in which thy weakness appeareth more than in desiring things? it is in the possessing, and in the using them.

Good things cease to be good in our wrong enjoyment of them. What nature meant pure sweets, are then sources of bitterness to us; from such delights arise pain, from such joys sorrow.

Be right in enjoyment, and it shall remain in thy possession; let thy joy be founded on reason, and to its end shall sorrow be a stranger.

The delights of love are ushered in by sighs, and they terminate in languishment and dejection, if the object thou burnest for nauseates with satiety; and no sooner hast thou possessed it, but thou art weary of its presence.

Join esteem to thy admiration, unite friendship with thy love; so shalt thou find in the end content so absolute, that it surpasseth rapture, tranquility more worth than ecstasy.

God hath given thee no good without its admixture of evil; but he hath given thee also the means of throwing off the evil from it.

As joy is not without its ally of pain, so neither is sorrow without its portion of pleasure. Joy and grief though unlike, are united. Our own choice only can give them to us uniquely.

Melancholy itself often giveth delight, and the extremity of joy is mingled with tears.

The best things in the hands of a fool may be turned to his destruction; and out of the worst the wise will find the means of good.

So blended is strength and weakness in thy Soul and body, O man! that thou hast not strength either to be good or to be evil entirely. Rejoice that thou canst not excel in evil, and let the good that is within thy Soul content thee.

The virtues are allotted to various stations. Seek not after impossibilities, nor grieve that thou canst not possess them all.

Wouldst thou at once have the liberality of the rich, and the contentment of the poor? or shall the wife of thy bosom be despised because she showeth not the learning of the widow?

If thy father sink before thee in the divisions of the country, can at once thy justice destroy him, and thy duty save his life?

If thou behold thy brother in the agonies of a slow death, is it not mercy to put a period to his life? and is it not also death to thus commit murder?

Truth is but one; thy doubts are of thine own raising. He who made virtues what they are, planted also in thee a knowledge of their pre-eminence. Act as Soul dictates to thee, and the end shall be always right.

CHAPTER IV

On the Insufficiency of Knowledge

If there is anything lovely, if there is anything desirable, if there is anything within the reach of man that is worthy of praise, is it not knowledge? and yet who is he that truly attaineth unto it?

The statesman proclaimeth that he hath it; the ruler of the people claimeth the praise of it; but findeth the subject that he possesseth it?

Evil is not requisite to man; neither can vice be necessary to be tolerated; yet how many evils are permitted by the connivance of the laws? how many crimes committed by the decrees of the council?

But be wise, O ruler! and learn, O thou who art to command the nations! One crime authorized by thee, is worse than the escape of ten from punishment.

When thy people are numerous, when thy sons increase about thy table; sendest thou them not out to slap the innocent, and to fall before the sword of him whom they have not offended?

If the object of thy desires demandeth the lives of a thousand, sayest thou not, I will have it? Surely thou forgetest that He who created thee, created also these! and their blood is as rich as thine, their Soul thine also.

Sayest thou, that justice cannot be executed without wrong? Surely, thine own words condemn thee.

Thou who flatterest with false hopes the criminal, that he may confess his guilt; art not thou unto him a criminal? or is thy guilt the less, because he cannot punish it?

When thou commandest to the torment him who is but suspected of ill, darest thou to remember, that thou mayest wrack the innocent?

Is thy purpose answered by the event? is the Soul in thee satisfied with his confession? Pain will enforce him to say what is not, as easy as what is; and anguish hath caused innocence to accuse herself.

That thou mayest not kill him without cause, thou dost worse than kill him; that thou mayest prove if he be guilty, thou destroyest him innocent.

O blindness to all truth! O insufficiency of the wisdom of the wise! Know when thy judge shall bid thee account for this, thou shalt wish ten thousand guilty to have gone free, rather than one innocent then to stand forth against thee.

Insufficient as thou art to the maintenance of justice, how shalt thou arrive at the knowledge of truth? how shalt thou ascend to the footsteps of her throne?

As the owl is blinded by the radiance of the sun, so shall the brightness of her countenance dazzle thee in thy approach.

If thou wouldst mount up into her throne; first bow thyself at her footstool; if thou wouldst arrive at the knowledge of her, first inform thyself of thine own ignorance.

More worth is she than pearls, therefore seek her carefully; the emerald, and the sapphire, and the ruby, art as dirt beneath her feet; therefore pursue her manfully.

The way to her is labour; attention is the pilot that must conduct thee into her ports. But weary not on the way; for when thou art arrived at her, the toil shall be to thee for pleasure.

Say not unto thyself, Behold, truth breedeth hatred, and I will avoid it; dissimulation raiseth friends, and I will follow it. Art not the enemies made by truth, better than the friends obtained by flattery?

Naturally doth man desire the truth; yet when it is before him he will apprehend it; and if it force itself upon him, is he not offended at it?

The fault is not in truth, for that is amiable, but the weakness of man beareth not its splendor.

Wouldst thou see thine insufficiency more plainly? view thyself at thy devotion! To what end was religion instituted, but to teach thee thine infirmities, to remind thee of thy weakness, to show thee that from heaven alone thou art to hope for good?

Doth it not remind thee that thy body is dust? doth it not tell it like unto ashes? And behold repentance; is it not built on frailty?

The shorter follies are the better: say not therefore to thyself, I will not play the fool by halves.

He that heareth his own faults with patience, shall reprove another with boldness.

He that giveth a denial with reason, shall suffer a repulse with moderation.

If thou art suspected, answer with freedom: whom should suspicion affright except the guilty?

The tender of heart is turned from his purpose by supplications, the proud is rendered more obstinate by entreaty, the sense of thine insufficiency commandeth thee to hear; but to be just, thou must hear without thy passions.

CHAPTER V

Misery

Feeble and insufficient as thou art, O man! in good; frail and inconsistent as thou art in pleasure; yet there is a thing in which thou art strong and unshaken. Its name is Misery.

It is the character of thy body, the prerogative of thy flesh: in thy thoughts alone it resideth; without these there is nothing of it. And behold, what is its source, but thine own physical passions?

He who gave thee these, gave thee also Soul to subdue them; exert it, and thou shalt trample them under thy feet.

Thine entrance into the world, is it not sorrowful? thy destruction, is it not glorious? Lo, men adorn the instruments of death with gold and gems, and wear them above their garments.

She who begetteth man, hideth her face; but she who killeth a thousand, is honoured.

Know thou, notwithstanding, that in this is error: Custom cannot alter the nature of truth; neither can the opinion of many destroy justice; the glory and shame are misplaced.

There is but one way for man to be created; there are a thousand by which he may be destroyed.

There is no praise, or honour, to him who giveth being to another; but triumphs and empire are the rewards of murder.

Yet he who hath many children, hath as many blessings; and he who hath taken away the life of another, shall not enjoy his own.

While the savage curseth the birth of his son, and blesseth the death of his father; doth he not call himself a monster?

Enough of evil is allotted unto man; but he maketh it more while he lamenteth it.

The greatest of all human ills is sorrow: too much of this thou art born unto; add not unto it by thine own perverseness.

Grief is natural to the mortal world, and is always about thee; pleasure is a guest, and visiteth thee but by thy invitation; use well thy mind, and sorrow shall be passed behind thee; be prudent, and the visits of joy shall remain long with thee.

Every part of thy body is capable of sorrow; but few and narrow are the paths that lead to delight that equal the joy of the Soul.

Pleasures can be admitted only singly; but pains rush in a thousand at a time.

As the blaze of straw fadeth as soon as it is kindled, so passeth away the brightness of joy, and thou knowest not what is become of it.

Sorrow is invited frequently, pleasure rarely; pain cometh of itself, delight must be purchased; grief is unmixed, but joy wanteth not its alloy of bitterness.

As the soundest health is less perceived than the lightest malady, so the highest joy toucheth us less deep than the smallest sorrow.

We are enslaved by anguish; we often fly from pleasure: when we purchase it, costeth it not more than it is worth?

Reflection is the business of man; a sense of his state is his first duty: but who remembereth himself in joy? Is it not in mercy then that sorrow is allotted unto us?

Man forseeth the evil that is to come; he remembereth it when it is past: he considereth not that the thought of affliction woundeth deeper than the affliction itself. Think not of thy pain except when it is upon thee, and thou shalt avoid what would hurt thee.

He who weepeth before he needeth weepeth more than he needeth: and why? but that he loveth weeping.

The stag weepeth not until the spear is lifted up against him; nor do the tears of the beaver fall, till the hounds are ready to seize him; man anticipateth death, by the apprehension of it; and the fear is greater misery, than the event itself.

CHAPTER VI

Of Judgment

The greatest bounties given to man are, judgment and will; happy is he who misapplieth not.

As the torrent that rolleth down the mountains, destroyeth all that is borne away by it; so doth common opinion overwhelm reason in him who submitteth to it, without saying, What is thy foundation?

See that what thou receivest as truth, be not the shadow of it! What thou acknowledgest as convincing, is often but plausible. Be firm, be constant, determine for thyself, so shalt thou be answerable only for thine own weakness.

Say not that the event proveth the wisdom of the action; remember man is not above the reach of accidents created by his will.

Condemn not the judgment of another, because it differeth from thine own; may not even both be in an error?

When thou esteemeth a man for his titles, and condemnest the stranger because he wanteth them, judgest thou not of the camel by his bridle? Think not thou art revenged of thine enemy when thou slayest him; thou puttest him beyond thy reach, thou givest him quiet, and thou takest from thyself all means of hurting him.

Was thy mother incontinent, and grieveth it thee to be told of it? if frailty in thy wife, and art thou pained at the reproach of it? He who despiseth thee, for it, condemneth himself. Art thou answerable for the vices of another?

Disregard not a jewel because thou possesseth it; neither enhance thou the value of a thing, because it is another's: possession to the wise addeth to the price of it.

Honour not thy wife the less, because she is in thy power: and despise him that hath said, "Wouldst thou love her less? marry her!" What hath put her into thy power, but her confidence in thy virtue? Shouldst thou love her less, for being more obliged to her?

If thou wert just of thy courtship of her; though thou neglectest her while thou hast her, yet shall her loss be bitter to the Soul in thee.

He who thinketh another best, only because he possesseth her; if he be not wiser than thee, at least he is more happy.

Weigh not the loss thy friend hath suffered, by the tears he sheddeth for it: the greater griefs are above these ex-pressions of them.

Esteem not an action, because it is done with noise and pomp; the noblest being is he that doth great things and is not moved in the doing of them.

Fame astonisheth the ear of him who heareth it; but tranquility rejoiceth the heart that is possessed of it.

Attribute not the good actions of another to bad causes: thou canst not know his heart; but the world will know by this that thine is full of envy.

There is not in hypocrisy more vice than folly; to be honest is as easy as to seem so.

Be more ready to acknowledge a benefit than to revenge an injury; so shalt thou be loved by more than hate thee.

Be willing to commend, and be slow to censure; so shall praise be upon thy virtues, and the eye of enmity shall be blind to thy imperfections.

When thou dost good, do it because it is good; not because men esteem it: when thou avoidest evil, fly because it is evil; not because men speak against it: be honest for love of honesty, and thou shalt be uniformly so; he that doth it without principle is wavering.

Wish rather to be reproved by the wise, than to be applauded by him who hath not understanding: when they telleth thee of a fault, they supposeth thou canst improve; the other, when he praiseth thee, thinketh thee like unto himself.

Accept not an offer for which thou art not qualified, lest he who knoweth more of it despise thee.

Instruct not another in that wherein thyself art ignorant; when he seeth it, he will upbraid thee.

Expect not a friendship with him who hath injured thee: he who suffereth the wrong, may forgive it; but he who doth it never will be well with him.

Nevertheless, ingratitude is not in the Soul of man; neither is his anger irreconcilable; he hateth to be put in mind of a debt he cannot pay; he is ashamed in the presence of him who he hath injured.

Repine not at the good of a stranger; neither rejoice thou in the evil that be falleth thine enemy: wishest thou that others should do thus by thee?

Wouldst thou enjoy the good-will of all men? let thine own benevolence be universal.

If thou obtainest it not by this, no other means could give it thee: and know, though thou has it not, thou hast the greater pleasure of having merited it; and in thy future states and beings shalt thou witness the marvels of thine acts in this state.

Chapter VII

Presumption

Pride and meanness seem incompatible; but man reconcileth contrarities: he is at once the most miserable and the most arrogant of all creatures.

Presumption is the bane of reason; it is the nurse of error; yet it is congenial with reason in us.

Who is there that judgeth not either too highly of himself, or thinketh too meanly of others?

Our Creator escapeth not our presumption: how then shall we be safe from one another?

What is the origin of superstition? and whence ariseth false worship? From our presuming to analyse about what is above our reach, to comprehend what is incomprehensible but to the self within.

Limited and weak as our mortal understandings are, we employ not even their little forces as we ought. We soar not high enough in our approaches to God's greatness; we give not wing enough to our ideas, when we enter into the adoration of divinity.

Man who fears to breathe a whisper against any earthly sovereign trembles not to arraign the dispensation of God; he forgetteth His majesty, and rejudgeth His judgments.

He who dareth not repeat the name of his prince without honour, yet blusheth not to call that of his Creator to be witness to a lie.

He who would hear the sentence of the magistrate with silence, yet dareth to plead with the Eternal, he attempteth to sooth him with entreaties, to flatter him with promises; to agree with him upon conditions; nay, to brave and murmur at him if his request is not granted.

Why art thou unpunished, O Man! in thy impiety, but that this is not thy day of retribution.

Be not like unto those who fight with the thunder; nor dare thou to deny thy Creator thy prayers because he chastiseth thee. Thy madness is on thine own head in this; thy impiety hurteth no one but thyself.

Why boasteth man, that he is favourite of his Maker; yet neglecteth to pay his thanks, is adoration for it? How suiteth such a life with a belief so haughty?

Man, who is truly but a mote in the wide expanse, believeth the whole earth and heaven created for him: he thinketh the whole frame of nature hath interest in his well-being.

As the fool, while the images tremble on the bosom of the water, thinketh that trees, towns, and the wide horizon, are dancing to do him pleasure; so man, while nature performs her destined course, believes that all her motions are but to entertain his eye.

While he courts the rays of the sun to warm him, he suposeth it made only to be of use to him; while he traceth the moon in her nightly path, he believeth she was created to do him pleasure.

Fool to thine own pride! be humble! know thou art not the cause why the world holdeth its course; for thee are not made the vicissitudes of summer and winter.

No change would follow if thy whole race existed not; thou art but one among millions that are blessed in it.

Exalt not thyself to the heavens; for, lo, the masters are above thee; nor disdain thy fellow-inhabitants of the earth, for that they are beneath thee. Are they not the work of the same hand? and breathe the same Soul?

Thou who art happy by the goodness of thy Creator, how darest thou in wantonness put others of his creatures to torture? Beware that it return not upon thee in compensation.

Serve they not all the same Universal Mother with thee? Hath He not appointed unto each its laws? Hath He not the care of their preservation? and darest thou to infringe it?

Set not thy judgment above that of all the earth; neither condemn as falsehood what agreeth not with thine own apprehension. Who gave thee the power of determining for others? or who took from the world the right of choice?

How many things have been rejected, which are now received as truths? how many now received as truths, shall in their turn be displaced? Of what then can man be certain?

Do the good that thou knowest, and happiness shall be unto thee. Labour is more thy business here than speculative thought.

Truth and falsehood, have they not the same appearance in what we understand not? what then but our Soul can determine between them?

We easily believe what is above our comprehension; or we are proud to pretend it, that it may appear we understand it. Is not this folly and arrogance?

Who is it that affirms most boldly? who is it that holds his opinion most obstinately? Even he who hath most ignorance; for he also hath most pride.

Every man, who layeth hold of an opinion, desireth to remain in it; but most of all he who hath most presumption. He contenteth not himself to betray his Soul into it; but he will impose it on others to believe in it also.

Say not that truth is established by years, or that in a multitude of beliefs there is certainty.

One human proposition has as much authority as another, if reason maketh not the difference.

Book Ten

▽

OF THE AFFECTIONS OF MAN, WHICH ARE HURTFUL TO HIMSELF AND OTHERS

CHAPTER I

Covetousness

RICHES are not worthy exclusive attention; there-fore selfish care of obtaining them is unjustifiable.

The desire of what man calleth good, the joy he taketh in possessing it, is grounded only in opinion. Take not up that from the vulgar; examine the worth of things thyself, and thou shalt not be covetous.

An immoderate desire of riches is a poison lodged in the mind. It contaminates and destroys everything that was good in it. It is no sooner rooted there, than all virtue, all honesty, all natural affection, fly before the face of it.

The covetous would sell his children for gold; his parent might die ere he would open his coffer; nay, he considereth not himself in respect of it. In the search of happiness he maketh himself unhappy.

As the man who selleth this house to purchase orna-ments for the embellishment of it, even so is he who giveth up peace in search of riches, in hope he may be happy in enjoying them.

Where covetousness reigneth, know that the mind is poor. Whoso accounteth not riches the principal good of man, will not throw away all other goods in the pursuit of them.

Whoso feareth not poverty as the greatest evil of his nature, will not purchase to himself all other evils in the avoiding of it.

Thou fool, is not virtue more worth than riches? is not guilt more base than poverty? Enough for his necessities is in the power of every man; be content with it, and thy happiness shall smile at the sorrow of him who heapeth up more.

Nature hath hid gold beneath the earth, as unworthy to be seen; silver hath she placed where thou tramplest it under thy feet. Meaneth she not by this to inform thee, that gold is not worthy thy regard, and that silver is beneath thy notice?

Covetousness burieth under the ground millions of wretches; these dig for their hard masters what returneth the injury; what maketh them more miserable than their slaves.

The earth is barren of good things where she hoardeth up treasure; where gold is in her bowels, there no herb groweth.

As the horse findeth not there his grass, nor the mule his provender; as the fields of corn laugh not on the sides of the hills; as the olive holdeth not forth there her fruits, nor the vine her clusters; even so no good dwelleth in the breast of him whose heart broodeth over his treasure.

Riches are servants to the wise; but they are tyrants over the mind of the fool.

The covetous serveth his gold; it serveth not him. He possesseth his wealth as the sick doth a fever; it burneth and tormenteth him, and will not quit him unto death.

Hath not gold destroyed the virtue of millions; did it ever add to the goodness of any?

Is it not most abundant with the worst of men? wherefore then shouldst thou desire to be distinguished by possessing it?

Have not the wisest been those who have had least of it? and is not wisdom happiness?

Have not the worst of thy species possessed the greatest portions of it? and hath not their end been miserable?

Poverty wanteth many things; but covetousness denieth itself all.

The covetous can be good to no man; but he is to none so cruel as to himself.

If thou be industrious to procure gold, be generous on the disposal of it. Man never is so happy as when he giveth happiness unto another.

CHAPTER II
Profusion

If there be a vice greater than the hoarding up of riches, it is the employing them to useless purposes.

He that prodigally lavisheth that which he hath to spare robbeth the poor of what nature giveth him a right unto.

He who squandereth away his treasure refuseth the means to do good; he denieth himself the practice of virtues whose reward is in their hands, whose end is no other than his own happiness.

It is more difficult to be well with riches, than to be at ease under the want of them.

Man governeth himself much easier in poverty than in abundance.

Poverty requireth but one virtue, patience, to support it; the rich if he hath not charity, temperance, prudence, and many more, is guilty.

The poor hath only the god of his own state committed unto him; the rich is instructed with the welfare of thousands.

He that giveth away his treasure wisely, giveth away his plagues: he that retaineth their increase, heapeth up sorrows.

Refuse not unto the stranger that which he wanteth, deny not unto thy brother that which thou wantest thyself.

Know there is more delight in being without what thou hast given, than in possessing millions which thou knowest not the use of.

CHAPTER III
Revenge

The root of revenge, is in the weakness of the Soul; the most abject and timorous are the most addicted to it.

Who tortures those they hate, but cowards? who murders those they rob but vile creatures?

The feeling and injury, must be previous to the revenging it: but the noble mind disdaineth to say, "It hurts me!"

If the injury is not below thy notice, he that doth it unto thee, in that, maketh himself so: wouldst thou enter the lists with thine inferior?

Disdain the man who attempteth to wrong thee; condemn him who would give thee disquiet.

In this thou not only preserveth thine own peace, but thou inflictest all the punishment of revenge, without stopping to employ it against him.

As the tempest and the thunder affect not the sun or the stars, but spend their fury on stones and trees below; so injuries ascend not to the Soul of the great, but waste themselves on such as are those who offer them.

Poorness of spirit will actuate revenge; greatness of Soul despiseth the offence; nay, it doth good unto him who intended to have disturbed it.

Why seekest thou vengeance, O man! with what purpose is it that thou pursuest it? Thinkest thou to pain thine adversary by it? Know that thyself feelest its greatest torments.

Revenge gnaweth the heart of him who is infected with it, while he against whom it is intended, remaineth easy.

It is unjust in the anguish it inflicts; therefore nature intended it not for thee; needeth he who hath been injured more pain? or ought he to add force to the affliction which another hath cast upon him?

The man who meditateth revenge is not content with the mischief he hath received; he addeth to his anguish the punishment due unto another; while he whom he seeketh to hurt, goeth his way laughing; he maketh himself merry at this addition to his misery.

Revenge is painful in the intent, and it is dangerous in the execution; seldom doth the axe fall where he who lifted it up intended; and lo, he remembereth not that it must recoil against him.

Whilst the revengeful seeketh his enemy's hurt, he oftentimes procureth his own destruction: while he aimeth at one of the eyes of his adversary, lo, he putteth out both his own.

If he attain not his end, he lamenteth it; if he succeed, he repenteth of it: the fear of justice taketh away the peace of his own mind; the care to hide him from it destroyeth that of his friend.

Can the death of thine adversary, satiate thy hatred? can the setting him at rest, restore thy peace?

Wouldst thou make him sorry for his offence, conquer him, and spare him: in death he owneth not thy superiority; nor feeleth he more the power of thy wrath.

In revenge there shall be a triumph of the avenger; and he who hath injured him, should feel his displeasure: he should suffer pain from it, and should repent him of the cause.

This is the revenge inspired from anger; but that which makes thee greatest, is contempt.

Murder from an injury ariseth only from cowardice: he who inflicteth it feareth that the enemy may live, and avenge himself.

Death endeth the quarrel; but it restoreth not the reputation: killing is an act of caution, not of courage; it is safe, but it is not honourable.

There is nothing so easy as to avenge an offence; but nothing is so honourable as to pardon it.

The greatest victory man can obtain, is over himself: he that disdaineth to feel an injury, restoreth it upon him who offereth it.

When thou mediatest revenge, thou confessest that thou feelest the wrong; when thou complainest, thou acknowledgest thyself hurt by it: meanest thou to add this triumph to the pride of thine enemy?

That cannot be an injury which is not felt; how then can he who despiseth it revenge it?

If thou think it dishonourable to bear an offence, more is in thy power; thou mayest conquer it.

Good offices will make a man ashamed to be thine enemy; greatness of mind will terrify him from the thought of hurting thee.

The greater the wrong the more glory is in pardoning it; and by how much more justifiable would be revenge, by so much the more honour is in clemency.

Hast thou a right to be a judge in thine own cause; to be a party in the act and yet to pronounce sentence on it? Before thou condemnest, let another say it is just.

The revengeful is feared, and therefore is hated; but he that is endued with clemency, is adored; the praise of his actions remaineth forever; and the love of the world attendeth him.

CHAPTER IV

Cruelty, Hatred, and Envy

Revenge is detestable! What then is cruelty? Lo, it possesseth the mischiefs of the other; but it wanteth even the pretense of its provocations.

Men disown it as not of their nature, they are ashamed of it as a stranger to their hearts: do they not call it inhumanity?

Whence then is her origin? unto what that is human oweth she her existence? Her father is Fear; and behold Dismay, is it not her mother?

The hero lifteth his sword against the enemy that resisteth; but no sooner doth she submit, than he is satisfied.

It is not in honour to trample on the object that feareth; it is not in virtue to insult what is beneath it: instruct the insolent, and spare the humble; and thou art at the height of victory.

He who wanteth virtue to arrive at this end, he who hath not courage to ascend thus into it; lo, he supplieth the place of conquest by murder, of sovereignty by slaughter.

He who feareth all, striketh at all: why are tyrants cruel, but because they live in terror?

The cur will tear the carcass, though he dared not look it in the face while living: the hound that hunteth it to the death, hanged it not afterwards.

Civil wars are the most bloody, because those who fight them are cowards: conspirators and murderers, because in death there is silence: is it not fear that telleth them they may be betrayed?

That thou mayest not be cruel, set thyself too high for hatred; that thou mayest not be inhuman, place thyself above the reach of envy.

Every man may be viewed in two lights: in the one he will be troublesome, in the other less offensive: choose to see him in that in which he least hurteth thee; then shalt thou do no hurt unto him.

What is there that a man may not turn into his good? In that which offendeth us most, there is more ground for complaint than hatred. Man would be reconciled to him of whom he complaineth: what murdereth he, but what he hateth?

If thou are prevented of a benefit, fly not into rage; the loss of thy reason, is the want of a greater.

Because thou art robbed of the cloak, wouldst thou strip thyself of thy undergarments also?

When thou enviest the man who possesseth honours; when his titles and his greatness raise thy indignation; seek to know whence they came unto him; inquire by what means he was possessed of them; and thine envy will be turned into pity.

If the same fortune were offered unto thee at the same price, be assured: if thou wert wise, thou wouldst refuse it.

What is the pay for titles, but flattery? how doth man purchase power but by being a slave to him who giveth it?

Wouldst thou lose thine own liberty, to be able to take away that of another? or canst thou envy him who doth so?

Man purchaseth nothing of his superiors but for a price; and that price, is not more than the value? Wouldst thou prevent the customs of the world? wouldst thou have the purchase and the price also?

As thou canst not envy what thou wouldst not accept, disdain this cause of hatred; and drive from thy Soul this occasion of the parent of cruelty.

If thou possessest honour, canst thou envy that which is obtained at the expense of it? If thou knowest the value of virtue, pitieth thou not those who have bartered it so meanly?

When thou hast taught thyself to hear the seeming good of man without repining, thou wilt hear of their real happiness with pleasure.

If thou seest good things fall unto one who deserveth them, thou wilt rejoice in it: for virtue is happy in the prosperity of the virtuous.

He who rejoiceth in the happiness of another, increaseth by it his own.

CHAPTER V

Heaviness of Heart

The Soul of the cheerful forceth a smile upon the face of affliction; but the despondence of the sad deadeneth even the brightness of joy.

What is the source of sadness, but feebleness of the mind? what giveth it power but the want of reason? Rouse thyself to the combat, and she quitteth the field before thou strikest.

She is an enemy to thy race, therefore drive her from thy heart; she poisoneth the sweets of thy life, therefore suffer her not to enter thy dwelling.

She raiseth the loss of a straw to the destruction of thy fortune. While she vexeth thy mind about trifles, she robbeth thee of thine attention to the things of consequence: behold, she but prophesieth what she seemeth to relate unto thee.

She spreadeth drowsiness as a veil over thy virtues; she hideth them from those who would honour thee on beholding them, she entangleth and keepeth them down while she maketh it most necessary for thee to exert them.

Lo, she oppresseth thee with evil; and she tieth down thine hands, when they would throw the load from off thee.

If thou wouldst avoid what is base, if thou wouldst disdain what is cowardly, if thou wouldst drive from thy heart what is unjust, suffer not sadness to lay hold upon it.

Suffer it not to cover itself with the face of piety; let it not deceive thee with a show of wisdom. Religion payeth honour to thy Maker; let it not be clouded with melancholy. Wisdom maketh thee happy; know then, that sorrow is to her looks a stranger.

For what should man be sorrowful; but for afflictions? Why should his heart give up joy, when the causes of it are not removed from him? Is not this being miserable for the sake of misery?

As the mourner who looketh sad because his tears are paid for; such is the man who suffereth his heart to be sad, not because he suffereth aught, but because he is gloomy.

It is not the occasion that produceth the sorrow; for, behold, the same thing shall be to another rejoicing.

Ask men if their sadness maketh things the better, and themselves will confess to thee it is folly; nay, they will praise him who beareth his ills with patience, who maketh head against misfortune with courage. Applause should be followed by imitation.

Sadness is against nature, for it troubleth her motions; lo, it rendereth distasteful whatsoever she hath made amiable.

As the oak falleth before the tempest, and raiseth not its head again, so boweth the heart of man to the force of sadness, and so returneth it unto its strength no more.

As the snow melteth upon the mountains, from the rain that trickleth down their sides, even so is beauty washed from off the cheeks by tears; and neither the one nor the other restoreth itself again for ever.

As the pearl is dissolved by the vinegar, which seemeth at first only to obscure its surface; so is thy happiness, O man! swallowed up by the heaviness of heart, though at first it seemeth only to cover its shadow.

Behold sadness in the public streets; cast thine eye upon her; avoideth she not every one? and doth not every one fly from her presence?

See how she droopeth her head, like the flower whose root is cut asunder? see how she fixeth her eyes upon the earth! see how they serve her to no purpose but for weeping!

Is there in her mouth discourse? is there in her heart the love of society? is there in her mind, reason? Ask her the cause, and she knoweth it not; inquire the occasion, and behold there is none.

Yet doth her strength fail her; lo, at length she sinketh into the grave; and no one saith, what is become of her?

Hast thou understanding, and seest thou not this? hast thou piety, and perceiveth thou not thine error?

God created thee in mercy: had He not intended thee to be happy, His beneficence would not have called thee into existence; how darest thou then to fly in the face of His Majesty?

While thou art most happy with innocence, thou dost Him most honour; and what is thy discontent but murmuring against Him?

Created He not all things liable to changes? and darest thou to weep at their changing? It is the law!

If we know the law of nature, wherefore do we complain of it? if we are ignorant of it, what should we accuse but our blindness to what every moment giveth us proof of?

Know that it is not thou that art to give laws to the world; thy part is to harmonize with them as thou findest them.

If they distress thee, thy lamenting it but addeth to thy torment.

Be not deceived with fair pretences, nor suppose that sorrow healeth misfortune. It is a poison under the colour of a remedy; while it pretendeth to draw the arrow from thy breast, lo, it plungeth it into thine heart.

While sadness separateth thee from friends, doth it not say, "Thou art unfit for conversation?" while it driveth thee into corners, doth it not proclaim that it is ashamed of thyself?

It is not in thy nature to meet the arrows of ill fortune unhurt; nor doth to bear misfortune like a man suffice; but thou must first also feel like one.

Tears may drop from thine eyes though virtue falleth not from thine heart: be thou careful only that there is cause, and that they flow not too abundantly.

The greatness of the evil is not to be reckoned from the numbers of tears shed for it. The greatest griefs are above these testimonials, as the greatest joys are beyond utterance.

What is there that weakeneth the mind like grief? what depresseth it like sadness?

Is the sorrowful prepared for noble enterprise? or armeth he himself in the cause of virtue?

Subject not thyself to ills, where there are in turn no advantages; neither sacrifice thou the means of good unto that which is in itself an evil.

▽   ▽   ▽

Book Eleven

▽

OF THE ADVANTAGES MAN MAY ACQUIRE
OVER HIS FELLOW-CREATURES

CHAPTER I

Nobility and Honour

FINE nobility resideth not but in the Soul; nor is there true honour except in goodness.

Crimes cannot exalt the man who commits them, to real glory; neither can gold make men noble.

When titles are the reward of virtue, when he is set on high, who hath served his country; he who bestoweth the honours hath glory, like as he who receiveth them; and the world is benefited by it.

Wouldst thou wish to be raised for men know not what? or wouldst thou that they should say, Why is this?

When the virtues of the hero descend to his children, his titles accompany them well; but when he who possesseth them is unlike unto him who deserveth them, lo, do they not call him degenerate?

Hereditary honour is accounted the most noble; but reason speaketh in the cause of him who hath acquired it.

He who, meritless himself, appealeth to the actions of his ancestors for his greatness, is like the thief who claimeth protection by flying to the pagod.

What good is it to the blind, that his parents could see? what benefit is it to the dumb, that his grandfather was eloquent? even so, what is it to the mean that their predecessors were noble?

A mind disposed to virtue, maketh great the possessor of it; and without titles it will raise him above the vulgar.

He will acquire honour while others receive it; and will he not say unto them, "Such were the men whom you glory in being derived from?"

As the shadow waiteth on the substance, even so true honour attendeth upon goodness.

Say not that honour is the child of boldness, nor believe thou that the hazard of life alone can pay the price of it: it is not to the action that it is due, but to the manner of performing it.

All are not called to the guiding of the helm of the state; neither are their armies to be commanded by every one; do well in that which is committed to thy charge, and praise shall remain upon thee.

Say not that difficulties are necessary to be conquered, or that labour and danger must be in the way to re-nown. The woman who is chaste, is she not praised? the man who is honest, deserveth he not to be honoured?

The thirst of fame is violent; the desire of honor is powerful; and he who gave them to use, gave them for great purposes.

When desperate actions are necessary to the public, when our lives are to be exposed for the good of our country, what can add force to virtue, but ambition?

It is not the receiving honour that delighteth the noble mind; its pride is the deserving it.

Is it not better men should say, "Why hath not this man a statue?" than that they should ask why he hath one?

The ambitious will always be first in the crowd; he presseth forward, he looketh not behind him. More anguish is it to his mind to see one before him, than joy to leave thousands at a distance.

The root of ambition is in every man; but it riseth not in all; fear keepeth it down in some, in many it is suppressed by modesty.

Honour is the inner garment of the Soul; the first thing put on by it with the flesh, and the last it layeth down at its separation from it.

It is an honour to thy nature when worthily employed; when thou directest it to wrong purposes, it shameth and destroyeth thee.

In the breast of the traitor ambition is covered: hypocrisy hideth its face under her mantle; and cool dissimulation furnisheth it with smooth words; but in the end men shall see what it is.

The serpent loseth not his sting though benumbed with the frost; the tooth of the viper is not broken though the cold closeth his mouth; take pity on his state and he will show thee his spirit; warm him in thy bosom, and he will requit thee with death.

He that is truly goodness, loveth virtue for herself; he disdaineth the applause for which ambition aimeth after.

How pitiable were the state of goodness, if she could not be happy but from another's praise? she is too noble to seek recompense, and no more will, than can be rewarded.

The higher the sun ariseth, the less shadow doth he cast; even so the greater is the goodness, the less doth it covet praise; yet cannot avoid its rewards in honours.

Glory, like a shadow, flieth him who pursueth it; but it followeth at the heels of him who would fly from it; if thou courtest it without merit, thou shalt never attain unto it; if thou deservest it, though thou hidest thyself, it will never forsake thee.

Pursue that which is honourable, do that which is right; and the applause of thine own conscience will be more joy to thee, than the shouts of millions who know not that thou deservest them.

CHAPTER II

Science and Learning

The noblest employment of the mind of man, is the study of the works of his Creator.

To him whom the science of nature delighteth, every object bringeth a proof of God; everything that proveth it, giveth cause of adoration.

His mind is lifted up to heaven every moment; his life is one continued act of devotion.

Casteth he his eye toward the clouds, findeth he not the heavens full of his wonders? looketh he down to the earth, doth not the worm proclaim "Less than omnipotence could not have formed me!"

While the planets perform their course; while the sun remaineth in his place; while the comet wandereth through the liquid air, and returneth to its destined road again; who but thy God, O man! could have formed them? what but infinite wisdom could have appointed them their laws?

Behold how awful their splendour! yet do they not diminish: lo, how rapid their motions! yet one runneth not in the way of another.

Look down upon the earth, and see her produce; examine her bowels, and behold what they contain; hath not wisdom and power ordained the whole?

Who biddeth the grass to spring up? who watereth it at its due season? Behold the ox croppeth it; the horse and the sheep, feed they not upon it? who is he that provideth it for them?

Who giveth increase to the corn thou sowest? who returneth it to the thousand fold?

Who ripeneth for thee the olive in its time? and the grape, though thou knowest not the cause of it?

Can the meanest fly create itself? or wert thou aught less than God, couldst thou have fashioned it?

The beasts feel that they exist, but they wonder not at it; they rejoice in their life, but they know not how it shall end: each performeth its course in succession; nor is there a loss of one species in a thousand generations.

Thou who seest the whole as admirable as its parts, canst thou better employ thine eye, than in tracing out thy Creator's greatness in them: thy mind, than in examining their wonders?

Power and mercy are displayed in their formation; justice and goodness shine forth in the provision that is made for them; all are happy in their several ways, nor envieth one the other.

What is the study of words compared with this? In what science is knowledge, but in the study of nature?

When thou hast adored the fabric, inquire into its use; for know the earth produceth nothing but may be of good to thee. Are not food and raiment, and the remedies for thy diseases, all derived from this source alone?

Who is wise then, but he that knoweth it? who hath understanding, but he that contemplateth it? For the rest, whatever science hath most utility, whatever knowledge hath least vanity, prefer these unto the others; and profit of them for the sake of thy neighbour.

To live, and to die; to command, and to obey; to do, and to suffer, are not these all that thou hast further to care about?

Morality shall teach thee these; the economy of life shall lay them before thee.

Behold they are written in thine heart, and thou needest only to be reminded of them; they are easy of conception; be attentive, and thou shalt retain them.

All other sciences are vain, all other knowledge is boast: lo, it is not necessary or beneficial to man; nor doth it make him more good, or more honest.

Piety of thy God, and benevolence to thy fellow creatures, are they not thy great duties? what shall teach thee the one, like the study of his works? what shall inform thee of the other, like understanding thy dependencies?

▽ ▽ ▽

Book Twelve

∇

MANIFESTATIONS OF KARMA

CHAPTER I

Prosperity and Adversity

EE that prosperity elate not thine heart above measure; neither depress thy mind unto the depths, because fortune beareth hard against thee.

Her smiles are not stable, therefore build not thy confidence upon them; her frowns endure not forever, therefore let hope teach thee patience.

To bear adversity well, is difficult: but to be temperate in prosperity, is the height of wisdom.

Good and ill are the tests by which thou art to know thy constancy; nor is there aught else that can tell thee the powers of thine own Soul; be therefore upon the watch when they are upon thee.

Behold prosperity, how sweetly she flattereth thee; how insensibly she robbeth thee of thy strength and thy vigour?

Though thou hast been constant in ill fortune, though thou hast been invincible in distress; yet by her thou art conquered, not knowing that thy strength returneth not again; and yet that thou again mayest need it.

Affliction moveth our enemies to pity; success and happiness cause even our friends to envy.

Adversity is the seed of well-doing: it is the nurse of heroism and boldness; who that hath enough, will endanger himself to have more? who that is at ease, will set his life on the hazard?

True virtue will act under all circumstances; but men see most of its effects when accidents concur with it.

In adversity man seeth himself abandoned by others; he findeth that all his hopes are centered within himself; he rouseth his Soul, he encountereth his difficulties, and they yield before him.

In prosperity he fancieth himself safe; he thinketh he is beloved of all that smile about his table; he groweth careless and remiss; he seeth not the danger that is before him; he trusteth to others, and in the end they deceive him.

The Soul can advise man in distress; but prosperity blindeth the truth.

Better is the sorrow that leadeth to contentment, than the joy that rendereth man unable to endure distress, and later plungeth himself into it.

Our passions dictate to us in all our extremes; moderation is the effect of wisdom.

Be upright in thy whole life; be content in all its changes; so shalt thou make thy profit out of all occurrences; so shall everything that happeneth unto thee be the source of praise.

The wise maketh everything the means of advantage; and with the same countenance beholdeth he all the faces of fortune: he governeth the good, he conquereth the evil; he is unmoved in all.

Presume not in prosperity, neither despair in adversity: court no dangers, nor meanly fly from before them: dare to despise whatever will not remain with thee.

Let not adversity tear off the wings of hope; neither let prosperity obscure the light of prudence.

He who despaireth of the end, shall never attain unto it; and he who seeth not the pit, shall perish therein.

He who calleth propserity his good; who hath said unto her, "With thee I will establish my happiness"; lo, he anchoreth his vessel in a bed of sand, which the return of the tide will wash away.

As the water that passeth from the mountains, kisseth in its way to the ocean, every field that bordereth the rivers; as it tarrieth not in any place; even so fortune visiteth the sons of men; her motion is incessant, she will not stay; she is unstable to the winds, how then wilt thou hold her? when she kisseth thee, thou art blessed; behold, as thou turnest to thank her she is gone to another.

CHAPTER II

Pain and Sickness

The sickness of the body affecteth even the spirit; the one cannot be in health without the other.

Pain is of all ills that which is most felt; and it is that which from nature hath the fewest remedies.

When thy constancy faileth thee, call to thy reason; when thy patience quitteth thee call in thy hope.

To suffer, is a necessity entailed upon thy nature, wouldst thou that miracles should protect thee from its lessons? or shalt thou repine, because it happeneth unto thee, when lo! it happeneth unto all? Suffering is the golden cross upon which the rose of the Soul unfoldeth.

It is injustice to expect exemption from that thou wert born to learn; submit with modesty to the laws of thy condition.

Wouldst thou say to the seasons, "Pass not on, lest I grow old?" is it not better to suffer well that which thou canst not avoid?

Pain that endureth long, is moderate: blush therefore to complain of it: that which is violent, is short: behold thou seest the end of it.

The body was created to be subservient to the Soul; while thou afflictest the Soul for the body's pain, behold thou settest the body above it.

As the wise afflicteth not himself, because a thorn teareth his garment; so the patient grieveth not his Soul, because that which covereth it is injured.

▽   ▽   ▽

SOME NOTES ON THE TERMS USED IN
THIS MANUSCRIPT

∇

As an aid to the reader the translator of the present modern copy of this book calls attention to the following distinctive terms and phrases used in the various chapters.

At the close of the preliminary instructions, the ancient form of authority is used: "Unto thee I grant the economy of life." This indicates that the original manuscript was used not only for individual and personal instruction, but was the official system used by the Masters of a school, and the giving of the instruction by the teacher was accompanied by a grant of power to apply the laws and principles on the part of the pupil.

In Chapter I, of Book I, we find reference to the "many lives," and "the compensation which The Law will exact." Here, we have reference to reincarnation and that law which is now more popularly known as the law of Karma.

In Chapter II, Book I, we note in the second paragraph the term "mortally ignorant." In modern mysticism that term would probably read *objectively ignorant* in contradistinction to the inherited subjective wisdom or natural wisdom of the Soul or inner-self.

In Chapter III, Book I, and many places throughout the manuscript, we find reference to "thy present state of being." Wherever this term is used, we may easily interpret the word *state* as meaning the *present incarnation* and, if this is kept in mind, it will make the statements much more instructive.

Also in the first paragraph of Chapter III, Book I, we find the principles of reincarnation illuminated by the statement that our action in the present incarnation will ordain or create or establish what we will be in the next incarnation. In the paragraph following that, is reference again to The Law, meaning once again the law of compensation or Karma. At the close of Chapter III in Book I the last words indicate that when the Soul of man is ready to reincarnate, it will attract to itself from the physical elements of this earth that physical body which it desires to animate. This is one of the fundamental principles of the teachings of the ancient Rosicrucians—that, just as we establish or attract for ourselves in this life what nature of incarnation we will have for our next "state"; so the Soul, just prior to rebirth on this plane, hovers about the earth plane and selects from among the many physical bodies being created by Nature, that one in such environment or in such physical state of nationality, locality, and other conditions, as will give the Soul the opportunity to carry on the work it has to do, or the lessons and experiences it has to learn. This is indeed a profound and interesting principle that modern mysticism has overlooked.

In Chapter I, of Book II, we find an excellent example of the ancient form of symbolism and mystical analogy. Here, *hope* is compared to the *rose in the bud*, and the *threatenings of fear* are likened unto a *cross,* upon which the rose is crucified. Aside from the excellency of the idea thus expressed, we find in it a veiled reference to the Rosicrucian symbol, which is a budding rose in the centre of a golden cross.

In the fifth paragraph of that same chapter, we find reference made to *the Soul,* and throughout the manuscript we are constantly impressed with another ancient idea that is rapidly becoming established as a very profound mystical principle, as well as a sound ecclesiastical law; namely that there is but *one Soul* in the universe, that which is of or from the consciousness of God and animates all mankind. That there is no separation of Souls or individual Souls in the physical individualities of mankind, but all have one Soul, a universal Soul, an undivided segment of which is in each living being. This is further presented in a beautiful way in the sixth and seventh paragraphs of Chapter I, in Book VIII, wherein we are told that after death the body remains as "perfect matter" or, in other words, a true state of material expression, although the Soul has left the body; which indicates that the Soul is not a part of the body, or even necessary to it, to make the body a material thing.

In Chapter II, of Book VIII, we have reference to *mind* and *Soul*, and their relation one to the other. In the first paragraph of this Chapter, the statement is made that the *mind resides in the Soul*. In various places we find the mind is distinguished from the *brain*, and *spirit* is also given a very distinct meaning in the same chapter.

In Chapter III, Book VIII, more light is thrown on the nature of the Soul with instructions as to how we can come to know the Soul. The statement in this Chapter that the Soul *was not born within us*, but was "concreated" for the body, and formed with the mind, indicates another profound belief that a Soul awaiting reincarnation leaves its spiritual realm and hovers close to the earth plane at a moment when it is ready to select a physical body that is just entering the first embryonic stages of development and growth.

In this same Chapter we have an interesting fact regarding animals, and are told that the Souls of other animals than man are not conscious of death or transition; that man alone possesses a Soul of such mind and consciousness as enable him to be conscious of such a state.

In Chapter IV, of Book VIII, we find in the seventeenth paragraph the interesting fact that death does not rob us of the opportunity to acquire knowledge; an indication that we may continue acquiring knowledge after transition and, presumably, while awaiting reincarnation. This illustrates the ancient belief that during the intervals between incarnations man is capable of sensing and communicating with other minds. However, this is not to be taken as a belief in those principles now presented by the spiritualistic doctrines, for the ancients and their successors today, especially the Rosicrucians, hold fast to the belief that such minds or personalities as are awaiting reincarnation do not put their spirit forms upon this earth plane. And that, while they may be able to make advanced mystics sense them, they do not clothe themselves with visible incarnate bodies until they reincarnate again.

Toward the close of Chapter III, in Book IX, we find the interesting statement that *strength* and *weakness* are *blended* in our Soul and body. In other words, that strength is an essential element of the Soul, and weakness an element of the body, because of its constant changing and mortality; and that, therefore, while the Soul is in the body strength and weakness are blended, and this prevents us from being entirely evil or entirely good. It is another form of the ancient statement that not until man has *ceased to learn* all the necessary lessons of life, and has learned how to resist all temptation, will he become completely good, though no longer having a body to clothe his Soul, and will live a spiritual life above this plane.

In Chapter V, of the same book, the first few paragraphs acquaint us with the further weaknesses of the physical body, and verify what has been previously said. This whole Chapter is interesting from this point of view. The close of Chapter VI, in this same book, reminds us again of the fact that as we build for ourselves in this incarnation, so shall we live in the next.

In Chapter II, of Book XII, we find in the first paragraph reference to the fact that disease of the physical affects the spirit of the body, or, in other words, that the essence called *spirit* is a material form of energy that is a part of the physical body, or,—a lower form of the universal essence; and that the spirit of the body is not the Soul-essence, which is immortal and cannot suffer or be affected by disease. Further on in that Chapter we find again reference to the golden cross and the rose of the Soul, and toward the last of this Chapter is a fitting closing to the whole book. We read that the body was created to be a *servant to the Soul* and that at no time should we permit the body or its faculties or mortal claims to rise above the *Mastership of the Soul*. This is sound mysticism and the keynote of the Rosicrucian teachings.

ROSICRUCIAN ORDER, AMORC.
PURPOSE AND WORK OF THE ORDER

▽

Because of the reference in this work to the Rosicrucians, and the Rosicrucian Order, I take this opportunity
to explain for those who might be interested regarding
this world-wide movement, the purpose of this Order and
how one may contact it further.

The Order is primarily a Humanitarian Movement,
making for greater Health, Happiness, and Peace in the
earthly lives of all Mankind. Note particularly that we
say in the *earthly lives* of men, for we have naught to do
with any doctrine devoted to the interests of individuals
living in an unknown, future state. The Work of Rosicrucians is to be done *here* and *now;* not that we have
neither hope nor expectation of *another* life after this, but
we *know* that the happiness of the future depends upon
what we do today for others as well as for ourselves.

Secondly, our purposes are to enable men and women
to live clean, normal, natural lives, as Nature intended,
enjoying *all* the privileges of Nature, and all benefits and
gifts equally with all of Mankind; and to be *free* from
the shackles of superstition, the limits of ignorance, and
the sufferings of avoidable *Karma.*

The Work of the Order—using the word "work" in
an official sense, consists of teaching, studying, and testing
such Laws of God and Nature as make our Members
Masters in the Holy Temple (the physical body), and
Workers in the Divine Laboratory (Nature's domains).
This is to enable the Brothers and Sisters to render *more*
efficient help to those who do not know, and who need
or require help and assistance.

Therefore, the Order is a School, a College, a Fraternity, with a laboratory. The Members are students and
workers. The graduates are unselfish servants of God to
Mankind, efficiently educated, trained, and experienced,
attuned with the mighty forces of the Cosmic or Divine

Mind, and Masters of Matter, space and time. This makes them essentially Mystics, Adepts, and Magi—creators of their own destiny.

There are no other benefits or rights. All members are pledged to give unselfish Service, without other hope or expectation of remuneration than to Evolve the Self and prepare for a *greater* Work.

For those who are unable to attend a local temple or lodge because of personal reasons or because of the fact that there might not be any in their immediate community, the National membership offers a personal, home study means. Instructions are sent in weekly lectures and lessons, especially prepared, and contain a summary of the Rosicrucian principles with such a wealth of personal experiments, exercises, and tests, as will make each member highly proficient in the attainment of certain degrees of mastership. The lectures are under the direction of the Imperator's staff. These correspondence lessons and lectures compose several degrees. Each degree has its own intitiation ritual to be performed by the member at his home in his own sanctum. Such rituals are not the elaborate rituals used in the temple lodges, but are simple and of practical benefit to the student. Those desiring further information regarding this beneficial form of study, need merely write to Scribe U. T. G., the Rosicrucian Order, San Jose, California, for further interesting literature that will be sent freely. Ask for the free book, "The Mastery of Life."

▽   ▽   ▽

The Rosicrucian Library

▽

Consists of a number of unique books
which are described in the following pages,
and which may be purchased from the

ROSICRUCIAN SUPPLY BUREAU
SAN JOSE, CALIF.   U. S. A.

VOLUME I

ROSICRUCIAN QUESTIONS AND ANSWERS WITH COMPLETE HISTORY OF THE ORDER

By DR. H. SPENCER LEWIS, F. R. C.

▽

THIS volume contains the first complete, authentic history of the Rosicrucian Order from ancient times to the present day. The history is divided into two sections, dealing with the traditional facts and the established historical facts, and is replete with interesting stories of romance, mystery, and fascinating incidents.

This book is a valuable one since it is a constant reference and guide book. Questions that arise in your mind regarding many mystical and occult subjects are answered in this volume.

For many centuries the strange, mysterious records of the Rosicrucians were closed against any eyes but those of the high initiates. Even editors of great encyclopedias were unable to secure the weird, fascinating facts of the Rosicrucian activities in all parts of the world. Now the whole story is outlined and it reads like a story from the land of the "Arabian Nights."

The book also outlines answers to hundreds of questions dealing with the history, work, teachings, benefits, and purposes of the Rusicrucian fraternity. It is printed on fine paper, bound in silk cloth, and stamped in gold. Price, postage prepaid, $2.00.

▽ ▽ ▽

VOLUME II

ROSICRUCIAN PRINCIPLES FOR THE HOME AND BUSINESS

By DR. H. SPENCER LEWIS, F. R. C.

▽

THIS volume contains such principles of practical Rosicrucian teachings as are applicable to the solution of the every-day problems of life in business and in the affairs of the home. It deals exhaustively with the prevention of ill health, the curing of many of the common ailments, and the attainment of peace and happiness as well as the building up of the affairs of life that deal with financial conditions. The book is filled with hundreds of practical points dealing especially with the problems of the average business man or person in business employ. It points out the wrong and right way for the use of metaphysical and mystical principles in attracting business, increasing one's income, promoting business propositions, starting and bringing into realization new plans and ideas, and the attainment of the highest ambitions in life.

"Rosicrucian Principles for the Home and Business' is not theoretical but strictly practical, and is in its fourth edition, having had a wide circulation and universal endorsement not only among members of the organization, who have voluntarily stated that they have greatly improved their lives through the application of its suggestions, but among thousands of persons outside of the organization. It has also been endorsed by business organizations and business authorities.

The book is of standard size, well printed, bound in silk cloth, and stamped in gold. Price, postage prepaid, $2.25.

▽   ▽   ▽

VOLUME III

THE MYSTICAL LIFE OF JESUS

By DR. H. SPENCER LEWIS, F. R. C.

▽

THIS is the book that thousands have waited for—the real Jesus revealed at last! It was in preparation for a number of years and required a visit to Palestine and Egypt to secure a verification of the strange facts contained in the ancient Rosicrucian and Essene Records.

It is a full account of the birth, youth, early manhood, and later periods of Jesus' life, containing the story of His activities in the times not mentioned in the Gospel accounts. The facts relating to the immaculate conception, the birth, crucifixion, resurrection, and ascension will astound and inspire you. The book contains many mystical symbols, fully explained, original photographs, and a new portrait of Jesus.

There are over three hundred pages with seventeen full chapters, beautifully printed, bound in purple silk, and stamped in gold.

Here is a book that will inspire, instruct, and guide every student of mysticism and religion. It is one of the most talked-about books ever written on the subject. Read it and be prepared for the discussion of it that you will hear among men and women of learning.

Sent by mail, postpaid, for $2.50.

VOLUME IV

THE SECRET DOCTRINES OF JESUS

By DR. H. SPENCER LEWIS, F. R. C.

DOES the Bible actually contain the unadulterated words of Jesus the Christ? Do you know that from 325 A. D. until 1870 A. D., twenty ecclesiastical or church council meetings were held, in which *man* alone decided upon the context of the Bible? Self-appointed judges in the four Lateran Councils expurgated and changed the sacred writing to please themselves. The Great Master's *personal* doctrines, of the utmost, vital importance to every man and woman, were buried in unexplained passages and parables. "The Secret Doctrines of Jesus," by Dr. H. Spencer Lewis, eminent author of "The Mystical Life of Jesus," for the first time *reveals* these *hidden truths*. Startling, fascinating, this new book should be in every thinker's hands. It is beautifully bound, illustrated, of large size, and the price, including postage, is only $2.50 per copy.

▽   ▽   ▽

VOLUME VI

A THOUSAND YEARS OF YESTERDAYS

By DR. H. SPENCER LEWIS, F. R. C.

HERE is a book that will tell you more about the real facts of *reincarnation* than anything that was ever written. It is a story of the soul, and explains in detail how the soul enters the body and how it leaves, where it goes, and when it comes back to earth again, and why.

The story is not just a piece of fiction, but a *revelation of the mystic laws* and principles known to the Masters of the Far East and the Orient for many centuries, and never put into book form as a story before this book was printed. That is why the book has been translated into so many forgein languages and endorsed by the mystics and adepts of India, Persia, Egypt, and Tibet.

Fascinating — Alluring — Instructive

Each who has read the book says that he was unable to leave it without finishing it at one sitting. The story reveals the mystic principles taught by the Rosicrucians in regard to reincarnation as well as the spiritual laws of the soul and the incarnations of the soul.

It is well printed, neatly bound with stiff cover, and worthy of a place in anyone's library.

Price, per copy, postage prepaid, only $1.00.

VOLUME VII

SELF MASTERY AND FATE WITH THE CYCLES OF LIFE

By DR. H. SPENCER LEWIS, F. R. C.

▽

THIS book is entirely different from any ever issued in America dealing with the secret periods in the life of each man and woman wherein the Cosmic forces affect our daily affairs.

The book reveals how we may take advantage of certain periods to bring success, happiness, health and prosperity into our lives, and it likewise points out those periods which are not favorable for many of the things we try to accomplish. It does not deal with astrology or any system of fortune telling, but presents a system long used by the Master Mystics in Oriental lands and which is strictly scientific and demonstrable. One reading of the book with its charts and tables will enable the reader to see the course of his life at a glance. It helps everyone to eliminate "chance" and "luck," to cast aside "fate" and replace these with Self Mastery.

Here is a book you will use weekly to guide your affairs throughout the years. There is no magic in its system, but it opens a vista of the cycles of the life of each being in a remarkable manner.

Well printed, bound in silk cloth, and stamped in gold to match other volumes of the Rosicrucian Library. Price, postage paid, $2.25.

▽   ▽   ▽

VOLUME VIII

ROSICRUCIAN MANUAL

By DR. H. SPENCER LEWIS, F. R. C.

▽

THIS practical book contains not only extracts from the Constitution of the Order of Rosicrucians, but a complete outline and explanation of all of the customs, habits, and terminology of the Rosicrucians, with diagrams and explanations of the symbols used in the teachings, an outline of the subjects taught, a dictionary of the terms, a complete presentation of the principles of Cosmic Consciousness, and biographical sketches of important characters connected with the work. There are also special articles on the Great White Lodge and its existence, how to attain psychic illumination, the Rosicrucian Code of Life with thirty laws and regulations, and a number of portraits of prominent mystics including Master K. H., the Illustrious.

The technical matter contained in the text and in the hundred or more diagrams makes this book a real encyclopedia of Rosicrucian explanations, aside from the complete dictionary it contains.

The "Rosicrucian Manual" is of large size, well printed, beautifully bound in red silk cloth, and stamped in gold. The fifth edition has been enlarged and improved in many ways. Price, postage prepaid, $2.35.

▽   ▽   ▽

VOLUME IX

MYSTICS AT PRAYER

Compiled by

MANY CIHLAR, *Austrian Philosopher and Mystic*

▽

THE first complete compilation of the famous prayers of the renowned mystics and adepts of all ages.

The book, "Mystics at Prayer," explains in simple language the reason of prayer, how to pray, and the Cosmic laws involved. You come to learn the real efficacy of prayer and its full beauty dawns upon you. Whatever your religious beliefs, this book makes your prayers the application not of words, but of helpful, divine principles. You will learn the infinite power of prayer. Prayer is man's rightful heritage. It is the direct means of man's communion with the infinite force of divinity.

"Mystics at Prayer" is well bound, embossed in gold, printed on art paper in two colors, with deckled edge and tipped pages, sent anywhere, postpaid, $1.10.

VOLUME XI

MANSIONS OF THE SOUL
The Cosmic Conception

By DR. H. SPENCER LEWIS, F. R. C.

▽

REINCARNATION! The world's most disputed doctrine. The belief in reincarnation has had millions of intelligent, learned and tolerant followers throughout the ages. Ringing through the minds and hearts of students, mystics, and thinkers have always been the words: "Why Are We Here?" Reincarnation has been criticized by some as conflicting with sacred literature and being without verification. This book reveals, however, in an astounding manner the many facts to support reincarnation. Quotations from eminent authorities, and from Biblical and Sacred works substantiate reincarnation. This volume PROVES reincarnation. It places it high above mere speculation. This book is without exaggeration the most complete, inspiring, enlightening book ever written on this subject. It is not a fiction story but a step by step revelation of profound mystical laws. Look at some of these fascinating, intriguing subjects:

The Cosmic Conception; The Personality of the Soul; Does Personality Survive Transition?; Heredity and Inheritance; Karma and Personal Evolution; Religion and Biblical View-points; Christian References; Between Incarnations; Souls of Animals and the "Unborn"; Recollections of the Past.

The book contains over three hundred pages, beautifully printed, neatly bound, stamped in gold; it is a valuable asset to your library, economically priced. Price, per copy, postage prepaid, only $2.35.

▽   ▽   ▽

VOLUME XII

LEMURA—THE LOST CONTINENT
OF THE PACIFIC

By WISHAR S. CERVE

▽

BENEATH the rolling, restless seas lies the mysteries of forgotten civilizations. Swept by the tides, half buried in the sands, worn away by terrific pressure, are the remnants of a culture little known to our age of today. Where the mighty Pacific now rolls in a majestic sweep of thousands of miles, there was once a vast continent. This land was known as Lemuria, and its people as Lemurians.

We pride ourselves upon the inventions, conveniences, and developments of today. We call them modern, but these ancient and long-forgotten people excelled us. Things we speak of as future possibilities, they knew as everyday realities. Science has gradually pieced together the evidence of this lost race, and in this book you will find the most astounding, enthralling chapters you have ever read. How these people came to be swept from the face of the earth, except for survivors who have living descendants today, is explained. Illustrations and explanations of their mystic symbols, maps of the continent, and many ancient truths and laws are contained in this unusual book.

If you are a lover of mystery, of the unknown, the weird—read this book. Remember, however, this book is not *fiction*, but based on facts, the result of extensive research. Does civilization reach certain height and then retrograde? Are the culture and progress of mankind in cycles, reaching certain peaks, and then returning to start over again? These questions and many more are answered in this intriguing volume. Read of the living descendants of these people, whose expansive nation now lies at the bottom of the Pacific. In the minds of these descendants is the knowledge of the principles which in by-gone centuries made their forbears builders of an astounding civilization.

The book, "Lemuria, the Lost Continent of the Pacific," is beautifully bound, well printed, and contains many, many illustrations. It is economically priced at $2.30, postpaid.

▽   ▽   ▽

Volume XIII

The Technique of the Master

The Way of Cosmic Preparation

By Raymund Andrea, F. R. C.

▽

A GUIDE to inner unfoldment! The newest and simplest explanation for attaining the state of Cosmic Consciousness. To those who have felt the throb of a vital power within, and whose inner vision has at times glimpsed infinite peace and happiness, this book is offered. It converts the intangible whispers of self into forceful actions that bring real joy and accomplishments in life. It is a masterful work on psychic unfoldment.

It is well bound in cloth, with deckled and tinted edged paper. Secure this treasure for yourself. Economically priced, postage prepaid, $2.00.

VOLUME XIV

THE SYMBOLIC PROPHECY OF
THE GREAT PYRAMID

By Dr. H. Spencer Lewis, F. R. C.

▽

THE world's greatest mystery and first wonder is the Great Pyramid. It stands as a monument to the learning and achievements of the ancients. For centuries its secrets were closeted in stone—now they stand revealed.

Never before in a book priced within the reach of every reader have the history, vast wisdom, and prophecies of the Great Pyramid been given. You will be amazed at the Pyramid's scientific construction and at the tremendous knowledge of its mysterious builders.

Who built the Great Pyramid? Why were its builders inspired to reveal to posterity the events of the future? What is the path that the Great Pyramid indicates lies before mankind? Within the pages of this enlightening book there are the answers to many enthralling questions. It prophesied the World War and the great economic upheaval. Learn what it presages for the future. You must not deprive yourself of this book.

The book is well bound with a hard cover, and contains all necessary charts and illustrations. Price only $2.25 with postage paid.

▽ ▽ ▽

VOLUME XV

THE BOOK OF JASHER

The Sacred Book Withheld

▽

BY WHAT right has man been denied the words of the prophets? Who dared expunge from the Holy Bible one of its inspired messages? For centuries man has labored under the illusion that there have been preserved for him the collected books of the great teachers and disciples—yet one had been withheld—"The Book of Jasher."

Within the hallowed pages of the great Bible itself are references to this lost book which have puzzled the devout and students for centuries. As if by Divine decree, the Bible appears to cry out to mankind that its sanctity had been violated, its truth veiled, for we find these two passages exclaiming: "Is not this written in the Book of Jasher"—Joshua x. 13; "Behold, it is written in the Book of Jasher"—2 Sam. i. 18.

Alcuin discovered this great book of the Bible written by Jasher. He translated it into English in 800 A.D. Later it was suppressed and then rediscovered in 1829, and once again suppressed.

But now we bring to you an actual Photographic Reproduction of this magnificent work, page for page, line for line, unexpurgated. This enlightening work bound in its original style, is priced at only $2.00 per copy, postage paid.

▽   ▽   ▽

VOLUME XVI

THE TECHNIQUE OF THE DISCIPLE

By RAYMUND ANDREA, F. R. C.

▽

"THE TECHNIQUE OF THE DISCIPLE" is a book containing a modern description of the ancient esoteric path to spiritual illumination, trod by the masters and avatars of yore. It has long been said that Christ left, as a great heritage to members of His secret council, a private method for guidance in life, which method has been preserved until today in the secret, occult, mystery schools.

Raymund Andrea, the author, reveals the method for attaining a greater life taught in these mystery schools, which perhaps parallels the secret instructions of Christ to members of His council. The book is enlightening, inspiring, and splendidly written. It is handsomely bound with a stiff board cover and the material of the cover is woven of silk thread and stamped in gold. Postage is paid on shipment to you. Priced at $2.15 per copy.

VOLUME XVII

MENTAL POISONING
Thoughts That Enslave Minds

By H. SPENCER LEWIS, Ph. D.

▽

TORTURED souls. Human beings, whose self-confidence and peace of mind have been torn to shreds by invisible darts— the evil thoughts of others. Can envy, hate, and jealousy be projected through space from the mind of another? Do poisoned thoughts like mysterious rays reach through the ethereal realm to claim innocent victims? Will wishes and commands born in hate gather momentum and like an avalanche descend upon a helpless man or woman in a series of calamities? Must humanity remain at the mercy of evil influences created in the minds of the vicious? Millions each year are mentally poisoned—are you safe from this scourge? "Mental Poisoning" is the title of a new book just written by Dr. H. Spencer Lewis, which fearlessly discloses this psychological problem. It is sensational in its revelations. Read it and be prepared.

This neatly bound, well printed book will be sent to you for the nominal price of only $1.25. It has been economically pro-duced so it can be in the hands of thousands because of the benefit it will afford readers.

Order yours today. Price includes postage.

▽   ▽   ▽

VOLUME XVIII

GLANDS—OUR INVISIBLE GUARDIANS

By M. W. KAPP, M. D.

▽

YOU need not continue to be bound by those glandular characteristics of your life which do not please you. These influences, through the findings of science and the mystical principles of nature, may be adjusted. The first essential is that of the old adage: "Know Yourself." Have revealed the facts about the endocrine glands—know where they are located in your body and what mental and physical functions they control. The control of the glands can mean the control of your life. These

[109]

facts, scientifically correct, with their mystical interpretation, are for the first time presented in simple, non-technical language, in a book which everyone can enjoy and profit by reading.

Mystics and metaphysicians have long recognized that certain influences and powers of a Cosmic nature could be tapped; that a Divine energy could be drawn upon, which affects our creative ability, our personality, and our physical welfare. For centuries there has been speculation as to what area or what organs of the body contain this medium—this contact between the Divine and the physical. Now it is known that certain of the glands are governors which speed up or slow down the influx of Cosmic energy into the body. What this process of Divine alchemy is and how it works is fascinatingly explained in this book of startling facts.

Dr. M. W. Kapp, long held in high esteem by the medical fraternity, and yet having a deep insight into the mystical laws of life and their influences on the physical functioning of the body, is author of this work.

INTRODUCTION BY H. SPENCER LEWIS, F. R. C., Ph. D.

Dr. H. Spencer Lewis—first Imperator of the Rosicrucian Order (AMORC), of North and South America, for its present cycle of activity, and author of many works on mysticism, philosophy, and metaphysics—wrote an important introduction to this book, in which he has highly praised it and its author.

The book is well bound with a hard cover; price only $1.30 with postage paid.

▽   ▽   ▽

VOLUME XIX

ALONG CIVILIZATION'S TRAIL

By RALPH M. LEWIS, F. R. C.

▽

DOES the dust of the ages disclose to the probing hands and peering eyes of Egyptologists more than they publicly disclose? Read of the mysterious nocturnal journey of an Egyptologist into the Valley of the Kings—the land of the dead.

What was the strange power or faculty that Sheikh Moussa el Howie possessed? Was it a psychic sense by which he detected and called forth from their places of concealment venomous reptiles and insects? Let the author reveal to you this eerie experience in an ancient temple on the Nile. Go on an expedition with these modern mystics. Tread with them over the crumbling bricks of a once mighty Babylon. Relive a life with one of the party in the great palace of Nebuchadnezzar. Realize with him the experiences of another existence.

Take part in the rituals and ceremonies of the hermetic brotherhoods of Europe, to which the author was introduced as a candidate. Journey along the ancient Nile. Cross absolute deserts. Investigate the sites of ancient civilizations and the mystery schools. Read of the mystical revival of an ancient ceremony in the King's Chamber—in the heart of the Great Pyramid—on the eventful day the Pyramid itself predicted.

"Along Civilization's Trail" is a book you will never forget; beautifully bound, illustrated with unusual *original photographs*. It is a book that will be prized by mystics and students everywhere. Price, $2.25, postpaid.

Printed in the United States
46453LVS00006B/96

Printed in the United States
46453LVS00006B/96

9 780766 138957